FOOD
FOR
SHOW
food on the go!

THE NEXT GENERATION

A collaboration of
Mount Sinai Community Foundation
and Sholom Home Auxiliary.

Minneapolis, Minnesota

Food for Show, Food on the Go!
First printing - 10,000, May 1983

Food for Show, Food on the Go! The Next Generation
Updated version - 7,500, November 2007

Published by
Mount Sinai Community Foundation and Sholom Home Auxiliary
3610 Phillips Parkway
St. Louis Park, MN 55426
952-939-1620

Printed by Shapco Printing
Minneapolis, Minnesota 55401

Graphic Design by Greer and Associates
Photography by Jill Greer
Styling by Judy Freeman

ISBN 978-1-60530-003-0

FOOD FOR SHOW

food on the go!

THE NEXT GENERATION

MOUNT SINAI COMMUNITY FOUNDATION

In The Beginning...

"Food For Show – Food On The Go"...was first published in 1983 by the Mount Sinai Hospital Auxiliary. It was a smash hit. Although Mount Sinai Hospital and the Auxiliary no longer exist, the legacy and tradition of Community Service, Philanthropy and Vision live on in the form of Mount Sinai Community Foundation, a Designated Endowment Fund of the Jewish Community Foundation.

Grant awards of up to $10,000 are considered during the one grant cycle each year, providing financial support to non-profit organizations for projects that Improve Health, Provide Medical Care or Strengthen Jewish Identity.

THE SHOLOM HOME AUXILIARY

Celebrating 100 Years...

"Food For Show – Food On The Go – The Next Generation" ...Sholom Home is a story of Love, Tradition, Hope, Dignity and Care, not only for the elderly, but also those in need of temporary assistance. Specialized programs, services and support for families and care givers are a high priority, along with a full calendar of social and recreational activities.

The cookbook is a collaboration of the Mount Sinai Community Foundation and Sholom Home Auxilliary, re-printing the 5th edition honoring Sholom's Centennial Year. Original recipes remain unchanged, and new generation recipes with specialty additions from prominent gourmet chefs add delicious flavor.

Sholom Home is Where the Heart Is
stir in
"Food For Show, Food on the Go! The Next Generation"
a perfect
Taste of Unity...Blend of Community...

COOKBOOK COMMITTEE "THEN"

CHAIRPERSON
Marcia Cherniack

TESTING CHAIRPERSON
Sandy Goodman

COORDINATORS
Fremajane Wolfson
Judy Harris

MARKETING CHAIRPERSONS
Muriel Wexler
Bonnie Kail

FOREWORD AND HISTORY
Arlis Grossman

TREASURER
Frances Finkelstein

EDITOR
Sue Zelickson

ASSISTANT EDITORS
Sheila Paisner
Delores Sigel

COOKBOOK COMMITTEE "NOW"

CHAIRPERSON
Beth Birke

PRINT PRODUCTION CHAIRPERSON
Sandie Kaster

TESTING CHAIRPERSON
Heide Mandel

VOLUNTEER CHAIRPERSON
Lori Kamin

TREASURER
Elissa Heilicher

CREATIVE CO-CHAIRPERSONS
Judy Freeman
Jill Greer

OPERATIONS CHAIRPERSON
Janie Lifson

CO-EDITORS AT LARGE
Marcia Cherniack
Sue Zelickson

ASSISTANT EDITORS
Carolyn Abramson
Delores Sigel
Heather Stesin

MARKETING COORDINATORS
Lori Kamin
Sue Harris

FORWARD AND HISTORY
Delores Sigel

SPECIAL ACKNOWLEDGEMENTS
Suzi Friedell
Greer and Associates
Shapco Printing

CONTRIBUTORS, TESTERS - THOSE WHO HELPED "THEN"

Ruth Aaron
Meryll Abelson
Myrna Abrams
Ruth Abry
Florence Alch
Lynne Alpert
Ida Altrowitz
Marian Altrowitz
Bonnie Axelson

Kerry Bader
Scott Bader
Arlene Badiner
Shirley A. Baker
Ardis Barnett
Linda Barrows
Joan Baskin
Patti Baskin
Joanne Bauman
Mabel Bauman
Edith Beirstein
Linda Benenson
Cathi Benson
Leona Berle
Charlotte Berman
David Berman, M.D.
Shirley Besikof
Joan Binder
Sura-Fraida Blatt
Arline Bloom
Percy Bloom
Andrea Bolger
Lou Ann Bongard
Linda Braufman
Carroll Britton
Ann Bronstien
Sylvia Bronstien
Cindy Brown
Ricki Butwinick

Susan Calof
Esther Capp
Ruth Cardozo
Edith Carlson

Harriet Cherniack
Marlys Cohen
Rusty Cohen
Verene Cohn
Jeanne Corwin
Sheila Corwin
Joan L. Cotroneo

Harriet Davis
Jodi Davis
Haddie Derechin
Laurie Derechin
Gayle Deshong
Marnie Desnick
Mitzi Diamond
Susan Diamond

Ceil Edwards
Wendy Engel
Marja Engler
Jan Ephraim

Cindy Fegley
Francine Feinberg
Frankie Filister
Harvey Filister
Irene Finberg
Marion Fisher
Linda Fiterman
Susan Fiterman
Sunny Floum
Pat Foulkes
Barbara Frank
Nancy Friedell
Margie Frishberg

Chicky Galinski
Pam Gallop
Hazel Garner
Minette Gaviser
Peni Gensler
Cindy Ginsberg
Barbara Gleekel
Lois Goldberg

Rivian Goldberg
Rivoli Golden
Diane Goldenberg
Eva Goldenberg
Judy Goldenberg
Cindi Goldfine
Cookie Goldman
Susan Goldman
Florence Goldstein
Renie Goldstein
Toni Goldstein
Annette Goodman
Beatrice Goodman
Lois Goodman
Shirley Goodman
Baylee Gordon
Jane Gordon
Margie Graceman
Etheldoris Grais
Babette Gross
Susan Grossman
Sylvia Grossman

Nene Haligman
Arlene Harris
Charlotte Harris
DeeDee Harris
Jane Harris
Jean Harris
Joye Harris
Natalie Harris
Sue Harris
M. Olivine Hayes
Linda Hechter
Pearl Heitke
Bea Herman
Valerie Herschman
Elliot Herstein
Min Himmelman
Jackie Hirsch
Ruth Hirsch
Arlene Hockenberg
Doris Hodroff
Diane Hoffman

CONTRIBUTORS, TESTERS - THOSE WHO HELPED "THEN"

Lori Holliday
Ethel Horne
Helen Horwitz
Linda Hyatt

Diane Ingber

Eva Jacob
Jane Jacobs
Joan Jaffee
Ellen K. Joseph

Ruth Kaiser
Susie Kane
Diane Kaplan
Helene Kaplan
Joy Kaplan
Lil Kaplan
Rose Kaplan
Sandy Kaplan
Vicki Kaplan
Raleigh Karatz
Stephanie Karon
Esther Kates
Anne Katz
Maxine Katz
Sherry Kehr
Delores Kelber
Risa Kessler
Marcella Killen
Roberta Kirschbaum
Doris Kirschner
Charlotte Klein
Marion Klein
Dianne Kline
Ruth Knelman
Donamae Koppelman
Peter Kordell
Divie Koval
Celia Krank
Myra Krank
Roberta Kravitz
Annetta Krelitz
Micki Kronick

Winnie Kuppe
Judy Kuretsky
Marcee Kutner

Joan LaBelle
Natalie LaBelle
Elaine Landy
Edith Latts
Janet Leavitt
Mimi Lebewitz
Miriam Leff
Roxanne Leopold
Ruth Levinson
Perri Levitus
Sharon Levitt
Dorothy Levy
Harriet Levy
Kay Levy
Lucky Levy
Marcia Levy
Sheila Lieberman
Miriam Link
Erma Lipschultz
Joni Lipschultz
Sybil Lipschultz
Sue London
Petrena Lowthian
Sandy Lurie
Carolyn Luther

Gail Machov
Renee Maisel
Joyce Malmon
Phyllis Mandel
Daisy Marcus
Helen Marhley
Marilyn Marker
Nancy Markowitz
Marjorie Marles
Ruth Mayeron
Leslie Melamed
Hiram Mendow
Josephine Mendow
Ardene Meshbesher

Naomi Meyerson
Ann Miller
Paulette Mitchel
Marlene Moscoe
Joyce Moscoe

Candy Nadler
Edith Nadler
Sooky Narvey
Nancy Nathanson
Annette Neff
Suzanne Nemer
Harriet Newman
Joan Noun

Barry Paisner
Charleen Paisner
Hy Paisner, M.D.
Martin Paisner, M.D.
Stephanie Paul
Joyce Peck
Mary Lou Peilen
Joyce Perlman
Enid Perimutter
Ferne T. Pesses
Jane Peterson
Bea Pink
Dorothy Pink
Lisa Pinsky
Jane Pistner
Marion Pollack
Marie A. Pudil

Gayle Rapoport
Susan G. Rappaport
Cheryl Ravich
Rollie Rinkey
Terry Rivard
Maryen C. Rivkin
Clara Roberts
Dona Rodich
Janice Rodkin
Sybil Robinson
Barbara Rosenberg

CONTRIBUTORS, TESTERS - THOSE WHO HELPED "THEN"

Phyllis Rosenblatt
Linda Ross
Tudie Ross
Gale Rothman
Pam Rothstein
Marilyn Rovner
Barbara Rubin
Elaine Rubin
Jana Rubin

Nancy Saliterman
Bertha Saisberg
Sylvia Samuels
Connie Sandler
Patti Sandler
Joanne Savitt
Bea Schimmel
Jack Schneck, M.D.
Marian Schneck
Eileen Schribman
Tina Schwartz
Lorraine Schweitzer
Carol Segal
Gloria Segal
Louise Segal
Lynne Segal
Robin Segal
Shelley Segal
Joyce Segalbaum
Marcia Shainock
Bernice Shapiro
Bonni Shapiro
Judy Shapiro
Rona Sher
Doris Sherman
Nancy Shiller
Darlene Schwartz
Lil Sigesmund
Shirley Silberman
Sara N. Silverstein
Marlen Simon
Susan Simon
Minnie Singer
Jessica Sipkins

Hazel Skarman
Maxine Smiley
Ethel Smith
Rollee Smith
Lynn Snyder
Sharon Snyder
Alicia Spitzberg
Ellyn Stein
Roz Steinfeldt
Elaine Steinman
Margie Stengold
Ione Stiegler
Jean Stillman
Liba Stillman
Marilyn Stillman
Ruth Stillman
Esther Straus
Abby Strauss
Cooky Strimling
Phyllis Sudit
Bruce Swanson
Dorothy Swatez
Annette Sweet
Betty L. Sweet

Marsha Tankenoff
Mollie Tankenoff
Paula Tankenoff
John C. Tidemann
Jean-Claude Tindiller
Joanne G. Topp
Mulvien Trach
Toodie Trestman
Karen Triebar
Rollie Troup
Margaret Tucker

Nancy Unterman

Peggy Vermes

Abby Walden
Lil Warschauer
Jackie Wartnick

Wanda Weick
Judie Weil
Margie Weil
Gail Weinberg
Judy Weiner
Joan Weinstein
Sue Weinstein
Phyllis Weisberg
Margery Weisman
Charlotte Weiss
Elaine White
Connie Wilensky
Goldie Wolf
Elizabeth Wolfson

Marcia Yugend

Margie Zats
Barry Zelickson
Penny Ziessman
Bonnie Ziskin
Sylvia Zouber

CONTRIBUTORS, TESTERS - THOSE WHO HELPED "NOW"

Carolyn Abramson
Sarah Anderson
Terry Appleman

Kim Balces
Linda Bartlett
Hannah Berck
Beth Birke
Peggy Bloom
Jamie Bonk
Lois Brand
Barbara Brooks

Marcia Cherniack

Carole Davidson
Gayle Deshong

Janet Flam
Judy Freeman
Suzi Friedell
Carol Furstneau

Jill Greer

Bonnie Halper
Sue Harris
Elissa Heilicher
Gloria Horowitz

Bruce Kahn
Lori Kamin
Susie Kane
Sue Kaplan
Sandie Kaster
Risa Kessler

Joan Labelle
Janet Leavitt
Debi Lehman
Harriet Levy
Rhoda Lewin
Helen Lifson
Janie Lifson
Beverlee Lobsinger

Heide Mandel
Roberta Mandel

Elaine Paul
Stephanie Paul
Lanie Paymar
Ina Pfefer

Janet Price
Bev Radin
Rollye Rinkey
Barbara Rosenzweig
Susan Roth

Carol Segal
Bernice Selwyn
Marilyn Shapiro
Doris Sherman
Delores Sigel
Shelli Stall Smith
Heather Stesin
Faye Stillman
Abby Strauss
Ellie Stropes

Sharon Torodor
Bonnie Tyszelman

Sue Zelickson

many thanks!

"GRANDMA'S CURE"

Rheumatism, Sniffles, The Gout and Psychoses
Lumbago, Hypertension, Rhinitis, Neuroses
Globus Hystericus, Heartburn, The Croup.

All boils down to Grandma's Cure...

Chicken Soup *see page 34*

TABLE OF CONTENTS

food for

Show ■ Showy for company

Go ■ Easy for busy days

Appetizers

TEX-MEX SPREAD

Show ■
Go ☐

2 (10½ oz.) cans bean dip, plain or
   jalapeno
1 c. dairy sour cream
½ c. mayonnaise
1 (1¼ oz.) pkg. taco seasoning mix
¼ tsp. garlic powder
3-4 ripe avocados
2 T. lemon or lime juice
½ tsp. salt
¼ tsp. pepper
8 oz. shredded sharp cheddar cheese
1 c. thinly sliced green onions
3 med. tomatoes, seeded and chopped
2 (3½ oz.) cans chopped ripe olives

In shallow 9x13-inch serving dish, spread bean dip. In small bowl, combine sour cream, mayonnaise, seasoning mix and garlic powder; spread over bean dip. Mash avocados, add lemon juice, salt and pepper; spread over the sour cream mixture. Sprinkle with cheese, onions, tomatoes and olives. Serve cold or heated with tortilla or taco chips.

12 servings

Removing tomato seeds keeps spread from getting watery. A large quiche dish is perfect for this amount. For a very spicy dip, add 2 (3 oz.) cans chopped green chiles.

a real tastemaker

MEXICAN APPETIZER

Show ■
Go ■

1 (8 oz.) pkg. cream cheese, softened
1 (15 oz.) can chili without beans
1 (3 oz.) can chopped green chilis
½-1 bunch green onions, diced
1 (3½ oz.) can pitted ripe olives, sliced
½-1 lb. Monterey Jack, cheddar or
    mozzarella cheese, shredded
Pitted ripe olive slices for garnish

Layer ingredients in order in 9-inch pie or quiche plate. Chill. Serve with crackers or taco chips

8 servings

GUACAMOLE

Show ■
Go ■

3 ripe avocados, peeled and mashed
½ tsp. garlic powder, or more to taste
1 T. medium salsa
salt and pepper to taste
1 tomato, chopped

Combine avocados, garlic powder, salsa, salt and pepper. Place in serving bowl. Sprinkle tomato on top. Refrigerate. Serve with taco chips, pita bread or fresh vegetables.

1 pint

So easy to prepare!

SALSA

Show ☐
Go ■

2 med. tomatoes, diced
1 med. onion, diced
¼ c. chopped green pepper
¼ c. chopped fresh parsley
1 clove garlic, crushed
½ tsp. salt
⅛ tsp. pepper
⅛ tsp. cumin powder
⅛ tsp. chili pepper to taste

Combine all ingredients in small bowl. Serve with tortilla chips

3 cups

CHILE CON QUESO

Show ■
Go ■

1 lg. onion, chopped
2 cloves garlic, chopped
2 T. oil
salt and pepper to taste
2 (4 oz.) cans green chiles, diced
1 (14 oz.) can whole peeled tomatoes,
    drained and chopped
1 (8 oz.) pkg. Monterey Jack cheese
1 (8 oz.) pkg. Velveeta cheese
1 (4 oz.) pkg. colby longhorn cheese

In 3-quart skillet, sauté onion and garlic in oil. Season with salt and pepper. Add chiles and sauté 2 minutes. Add tomatoes and simmer 10 minutes. Cut cheese into chunks and add to warm sauce. Cook on low heat until cheese is almost melted, but still is a little chunky.

Serve in a chafing dish with tortilla chips for dipping. For nachos, spread melted mixture on tortilla chips. Bake at 350° for about 5 minutes or until bubbly.

1 quart

Some like it hot!

ROSEWOOD ROOM GRAVLAX AND DILL SAUCE

Show ■
Go ☐

1½-2 lb. fresh boned salmon side
¼ c. brown sugar
¼ c. salt
dash white pepper
1 tsp. ground celery seed
1 tsp. fennel seed
½ c. finely chopped fresh dill
1 c. oil

Dill sauce:
3 egg yolks
1 c. oil
¼ c. Dijon mustard
½ c. brown sugar
2 T. finely chopped fresh dill
Tabasco
salt
Worcestershire sauce

Place salmon in shallow pan, skin side down. Combine sugar, salt, pepper, celery seed and fennel seed; sprinkle over salmon. Cover with dill. Slowly pour oil over fish, cover tightly and refrigerate 7–12 days.

Make dill sauce by beating egg yolks until creamy. Slowly add oil, beating constantly to thicken. Add mustard, sugar and dill; season to taste with remaining ingredients. To serve, remove fish from pan and scrape away dill and spices. Pat dry. Cut salmon into thin diagonal slices with electric knife. Serve with dill sauce and black or rye bread.

10 to 12 servings

DILLED SHRIMP APPETIZER

Show ■
Go ■

1½ c. mayonnaise
⅓ c. lemon juice (or more to taste)
¼ c. sugar
½ c. dairy sour cream
1 lg. red onion, sliced
2 T. dill weed
¼ tsp. salt
2 T. capers
2 lbs. shrimp, cooked

Mix all ingredients, stirring in shrimp last. Refrigerate overnight. Serve with toothpicks.

8-10 servings

May be prepared up to 48 hours in advance.

SPICY PICKLED SHRIMP

Show ■
Go □

1 lb. med. shrimp
2 lg. onions, chopped
3 cloves garlic, chopped
½ c. olive oil
½ c. cider vinegar
¼ c. white wine
5 fresh jalapeno peppers, sliced or 1
   (4 oz.) can jalepeno peppers or
   green chiles
few dashes Tabasco sauce (optional)
1 c. chopped green onions
lettuce
4-6 radishes, sliced
8-10 green olives

Clean and shell shrimp leaving tails on. In a large skillet over medium heat, sauté onions and garlic in oil for 3 minutes. Add shrimp and stir-fry until pink. Remove and place in medium size bowl. Add vinegar, wine, peppers, Tabasco and green onions. Cover tightly and refrigerate at least 24 hours, stirring occasionally. Serve on lettuce-lined platter garnished with radish slices and green olives.

6-8 servings

NANTUCKET CRAB MOLD

Show ■
Go □

1 (10¾ oz.) can tomato soup
1 envelope unflavored gelatin
¼ c. cold water
1 (8 oz.) pkg. cream cheese, softened
¾ c. mayonnaise
½ c. finely chopped onions
¾ c. chopped celery
2 dashes Tabasco
½ tsp. paprika
1 tsp. Worcestershire sauce
2 tsp. white horseradish
2 (6 oz.) pkgs. frozen snow crab, thawed

Bring soup to a boil. Remove from heat. Soften gelatin in water. Add to soup; stir until gelatin is dissolved. Cool. Beat cream cheese until smooth. Add soup mixture and beat until combined. Add remaining ingredients. Pour into a greased 6-cup mold. Refrigerate overnight. Unmold and serve with crackers, party rye or pumpernickel bread.

10-12 servings

LE GRANDE TUNA BALL

Show ■
Go ■

1 (8 oz.) pkg. cream cheese, softened
1 T. chopped onion
dash Tabasco
¼ tsp. salt
1 (7 oz.) can tuna, well drained and flaked
¼ c. chopped ripe olives
¼ c. chopped parsley
1 c. shredded cheddar cheese

Mix together cream cheese, onion, Tabasco and salt. Add tuna, olives and half of the parsley. Shape mixture into a ball. Combine remaining parsley and cheddar cheese. Roll ball in parsley mixture and refrigerate for several hours or overnight. Serve with crackers.

8 servings

EGG SALAD MOLD

Show ■
Go ☐

12 hard-cooked eggs, chopped
1 c. Miracle Whip or mayonnaise
¼ c. minced onion
2 T. prepared mustard
1 tsp. salt
1 tsp. pepper
2 envelopes unflavored gelatin
½ c. cold water
½ c. plus 1 T. whipping cream, whipped
1 c. dairy sour cream
dash onion salt
12 olives
12 cherry tomatoes
Seafood Dressing (see index)

Combine eggs, Miracle Whip, onion, mustard, salt and pepper together and set aside. Sprinkle gelatin over water in small saucepan and heat slowly until dissolved. Cool slightly, mix with egg mixture and refrigerate. Fold whipped cream into egg mixture and spread into a greased 6½-cup ring mold. Refrigerate overnight.

Unmold on serving platter and frost with sour cream that has been seasoned with a dash of onion salt. Garnish with olives and cherry tomatoes. Serve with crackers or party rye. Place bowl of Seafood Dressing in center of mold.

10-12 servings

ARTICHOKE SQUARES

Show ■
Go ■

2 (6 oz.) jars marinated artichoke hearts
2 med. onions, chopped
1 clove garlic, crushed
4 eggs, beaten
½ c. bread crumbs
¼ tsp. salt
½ tsp. pepper
½ tsp. oregano
½ tsp. Tabasco
8 oz. shredded sharp cheddar cheese
2 T. chopped parsley
grated parmesan cheese
paprika

Drain marinade from one jar of artichokes into skillet. Discard remaining marinade. Chop artichokes and set aside. Sauté onions and garlic in marinade for 5 minutes. Combine eggs, crumbs, seasonings, cheddar cheese, parsley and sautéed onions. Add artichokes. Pour into greased 8x8-inch pan. Bake at 325° for 30 minutes or until set. Sprinkle with parmesan cheese and paprika last five minutes of baking. Cut into squares and serve.

8-10 serving

HOT SPINACH SPHERES

Show ■
Go ☐

4 lg. eggs, beaten
2 (10 oz.) pkg. frozen chopped spinach,
    thawed and well drained
1 T. finely minced onion
¾ c. butter, melted
¾ c. grated parmesan cheese
½ tsp. salt
¼ tsp. pepper
½ tsp. thyme
¼ tsp. nutmeg
dash Tabasco
2 ½ c. crumbled herb-seasoned stuffing mix

Combine eggs, spinach, onion, butter, cheese, salt, pepper, thyme, nutmeg and Tabasco. When well blended, add stuffing mix. Stir and let stand 20 minutes or until slightly firm. Shape into walnut-size balls and place on ungreased baking sheet. Bake at 350° for 20 minutes.

60 pieces

May be prepared ahead and frozen. Reheat at 350° for 10-15 minutes.

COLD SPINACH MOUSSE

Show ■
Go □

2 T. oil
3 (10 oz.) pkgs. frozen chopped spinach
1 tsp. salt
½ tsp. pepper
½ tsp. nutmeg
1 sm. onion, grated
1 c. mayonnaise
1 T. lemon juice
2 envelopes unflavored gelatin
¼ c. water
1 c. whipping cream, whipped

Green Mayonnaise:
12 watercress leaves
6 sprigs parsley
13 spinach leaves
2 c. mayonnaise

Brush 6-cup ring mold with oil. Cook spinach according to package directions. Drain well; squeeze out moisture and chop finely. In large bowl, combine salt, pepper, nutmeg, onion, mayonnaise and lemon juice. In small saucepan, dissolve gelatin in water over low heat. Fold gelatin into whipped cream and combine with spinach mixture. Pour into mold and refrigerate 2 hours.

For green mayonnaise, drop watercress, parsley and spinach leaves into boiling water. Blanch 1 minute. Drain and rinse in cold water. Squeeze dry; chop and combine with mayonnaise. To serve mousse, unmold on serving platter and top with green mayonnaise.

6-8 servings

CHOPPED EGGPLANT

Show ■
Go □

1 med. eggplant
1 med. onion, chopped
2 cloves garlic
1 sm. green pepper, chopped
1 sm. tomato, chopped
1 tsp. salt
dash pepper
3 T. oil
1 T. vinegar

Prick eggplant and bake at 400° for 30 minutes or until soft. Cool and peel. Chop eggplant in blender or food processor. Combine with remaining ingredients; cover and refrigerate at least 24 hours. Serve chilled with crackers or cocktail rye.

8-10 servings

EGGPLANT CAVIAR

Show ■
Go ☐

1 med. eggplant, unpeeled and diced
1 lg. onion, chopped
½ green pepper, chopped
2 cloves garlic, crushed
⅓ c. olive oil
1 tsp. salt
½ tsp. pepper
½ tsp. oregano
½ tsp. basil
1 T. sugar
1 (6 oz.) can tomato paste
¼ c. water
¼ c. vinegar
½ c. sliced pimento stuffed green olives
1 (4 oz.) can mushrooms, drained and
    chopped
¼ c. capers (optional)

Combine eggplant, onion, green pepper, garlic and oil in large skillet. Cover and simmer for 10 minutes. Add remaining ingredients; cover and simmer until eggplant is cooked but not mushy, about 20 minutes. Chill and serve cold in lettuce-lined bowl as cocktail spread with favorite rye bread or crackers.

1 quart

CUCUMBER DIP

Show ■
Go ■

1 (8 oz.) pkg. cream cheese, softened
1 sm. unpeeled cucumber, chopped
¼ c. chopped green onions
garlic salt

Mix all ingredients together by hand. Cover and refrigerate overnight. Serve with cut-up vegetables.

10-12 servings

ANCHOVY SPREAD

Show ■
Go ■

1 (8 oz.) pkg. cream cheese, softened
2 (2 oz.) flat cans anchovies, chopped
1 tsp. lemon juice
dash Worcestershire sauce
1 generous T. Miracle Whip

Blend all ingredients together by hand. Refrigerate for several hours. Remove 1 hour before serving. Serve with rye bread.

10-12 servings

CHICKEN LIVER PATÉ

Show ■
Go ☐

2½ T. butter
5-6 shallots, peeled and finely chopped
1 bay leaf
1 lb. chicken livers
3 cloves garlic, chopped
½ c. cognac
2 c. whipping cream
3 T. finely chopped parsley
salt and pepper

In a skillet over low heat, melt butter and cook shallots with bay leaf until soft. Do not brown. Turn heat to high and cook until translucent. Add chicken livers and garlic; sauté quickly on both sides.

In a small saucepan, heat cognac; pour over livers and ignite mixture with a match. Cook 1½ minutes, watching carefully. Douse flame by covering with lid. In a large saucepan heat cream; add to livers and bring to boil. Discard bay leaf. Add 2 tablespoons of parsley, and salt and pepper to taste. Place ingredients in food processor and puree. Mixture will be soft. Spoon paté into individual ramekins or 1-quart serving dish and refrigerate overnight. Before serving, garnish with remaining parsley. May be frozen.

1 quart

HERB CHEESE SPREAD

Show □
Go ■

1 (3 oz.) pkg. cream cheese, softened
¼ tsp. chervil
¼ tsp. chives
¼ tsp. chopped parsley
garlic powder to taste

Blend ingredients together. Serve with crackers.

¾ cup

ANTIPASTO TO GO

Show ■
Go ■

1½ c. chopped ripe olives
1 c. chopped pimento stuffed green olives
3 med. tomatoes, chopped
6 green onions, chopped
1 med. green pepper, chopped
2 T. tarragon vinegar
1 T. oil
Tabasco to taste

Combine all ingredients and place in bowl. Refrigerate for 24-48 hours. Drain off some of the liquid before serving.

1 quart

HERRING ANTIPASTO

Show ■
Go ■

1 (16 oz.) jar herring in wine sauce
1 med. green pepper, chopped
1 med. red onion, chopped
1 (2¼ oz.) can sliced ripe olives
1 (6 oz.) jar marinated artichokes, drained
1 (12 oz.) jar Bennetts chili sauce

Drain and cut herring into small pieces. Place in bowl and add green pepper, onions, olives and artichokes. Add chili sauce. Cover and refrigerate 2 hours or overnight. Serve plain or with crackers or cocktail breads.

4 cups

FANCY ANTIPASTO

Show ■
Go ☐

1 c. ketchup
1 c. chili sauce
1 c. water
½ c. olive oil
½ c. tarragon vinegar
½ c. lemon juice
1 clove garlic, crushed
2 T. brown sugar
1 T. Worcestershire sauce
1 T. prepared horseradish
salt to taste
dash cayenne
½ head cauliflower, cut into
    flowerets
3-5 carrots, sliced diagonally
    into 1½-inch pieces
2-4 ribs celery, sliced diagonally
    into 1½-inch pieces
1 (6 oz.) jar artichoke hearts,
    drained, cut into halves
½ lb. whole fresh mushrooms
1 (8 oz.) jar pepperoncini, drained
1 (2 oz.) jar stuffed olives, drained
2 (7 oz.) cans tuna, drained

Into large saucepan combine ketchup, chili sauce, water, oil, vinegar and lemon juice. Season with garlic, brown sugar, Worcestershire, horseradish, salt and cayenne. Bring to a boil and simmer a few minutes. Add the vegetables and simmer 20 minutes or until vegetables are tender. Add tuna and simmer a few minutes longer. Cool. Cover and refrigerate. Serve with crackers.

3 quarts

Will keep two weeks in refrigerator.

A little taste of Italy

PARTY HERRING SALAD

Show ■
Go ■

1 (16 oz.) jar pickled herring fillets, drained
2 apples, peeled and chopped
2 navel oranges, peeled and chopped
1 sm. red onion, chopped
8 oz. dairy sour cream

Cut herring into small pieces and place in a bowl. Add apples, oranges, onion and sour cream; mix well. Cover and refrigerate until thoroughly chilled. Serve with rye bread or crackers.

16 servings

Show ■
Go ■

CHUTNEY-CURRY CHEESE SPREAD

2 (8 oz.) pkgs. cream cheese
1 c. shredded sharp cheddar cheese
½-1 tsp. curry powder
2 T. sherry
1 (9 oz.) bottle mango chutney
5 green onions, finely chopped

In double boiler, heat cream cheese, cheddar cheese, curry powder and sherry until cheese melts. Spread on large round plate. Cover and chill. Before serving, spread chutney over mixture and sprinkle with green onions. Serve with crackers. May be prepared a day ahead.

12-14 servings

Show ■
Go ■

WITH A BRICK OF CREAM CHEESE

1 (sm. or lg.) brick cream cheese
soy sauce and sesame seeds
    or
caviar and chopped green onions and
    sieved cooked egg yolks
    or
Spiced Green Pepper Jelly
    (see index)

Place brick of cheese on a serving dish that has sides. Cover with topping of soy sauce sprinkled with sesame seeds OR caviar sprinkled with green onions and egg yolks OR Spiced Green Pepper Jelly; serve with your favorite crackers or rye toast.

4-8 servings

CHEESE STICKS

Show ■
Go □

¾ c. plus 2 T. butter
2 c. flour
½ tsp. salt
1 c. shredded Swiss cheese
3 T. grated parmesan cheese
1 egg, beaten
2½ T. milk
1 egg, beaten
poppy seeds

In food processor or mixer, blend butter, flour and salt until crumbly. Add cheeses, 1 egg and milk, being careful not to over blend. Refrigerate dough about 30 minutes. Cut in half and roll out each part into an 8x12-inch rectangle about ¼ inch thick. Using a sharp knife or pastry wheel, cut into 3x½-inch strips. Place on foil-lined ungreased cookie sheets. Brush with beaten egg and sprinkle with poppy seeds. Bake at 375° for 12 minutes or until golden brown.

7-8 dozen

May be frozen baked or unbaked. Do not thaw before baking.

BAKED GOUDA

Show ■
Go ■

1 (8 oz.) pkg. refrigerated crescent
　　style dinner rolls
1 (7 oz.) Gouda cheese
1 egg white, beaten
sesame seeds

Using finger, smooth out perforated marks on dough to form solid rectangle. Remove casing from Gouda and place cheese in center of dough. Bring up all corners of dough to totally encase cheese, making sure all openings are sealed. Brush top with egg white and sprinkle with sesame seeds. Place on ungreased cookie sheet. Bake at 375° for 30 minutes or until golden.

Allow to sit a few minutes before cutting into wedges. For a variation, before closing the cheese, coat with several teaspoons of any style prepared mustard.

4-6 servings

HOT AND SAUCY SALAMI

Show ■
Go ■

1 (2 lb.) Kosher salami or bologna
½ c. tomato soup
½ c. vinegar
½ c. mustard
½ c. sugar
½ c. butter, melted
3 egg yolks, beaten

Remove casing from salami, score top and place in a shallow baking dish. In saucepan combine remaining ingredients and cook until thick, stirring constantly, about 20 minutes. Brush the sauce over salami. Bake uncovered at 350° for 1 hour or until crusty, basting occasionally. Serve remaining sauce on the side.

12 servings

BAKED BOLOGNA OR SALAMI

Show ■
Go ■

1 (1 lb.) Kosher bologna or salami, skin on
½ c. apricot jam
¼ c. brandy

Cut bologna or salami in half lengthwise. Place in a shallow pan, rounded side up. Score top in several places. Mix together jam and brandy. Brush ½ mixture on bologna. Bake at 350° for 1 hour, basting often with remaining mixture. Slice and serve. May cut bologna or salami in chunks; pour on mixture and bake.

4-6 servings

May add 2 tablespoons prepared mustard to jam and brandy mixture.

No Baloney!

MEATBALLS SUPREME

Show ■
Go ☐

2 lbs. ground beef
½ c. water
1 egg
¼-½ envelope dry onion soup mix
½ c. bread crumbs
2 tsp. garlic powder (or to taste)
1 (16 oz.) can whole cranberry sauce
2 c. ketchup
½-1 c. water

In a large bowl, combine beef, water, egg, onion soup, bread crumbs and garlic powder. Shape into balls and place in a covered roasting pan. In a saucepan, combine cranberry sauce, ketchup and water. Bring to a boil and simmer 5 minutes. Pour over meat balls. Cover and bake at 350° for 2 hours. Uncover and bake 1 more hour.

The meatballs freeze well. Bake 2 hours, cool and freeze. Defrost and reheat for 1 hour.

40 meatballs

WATERCRESS SANDWICHES

Show ■
Go ■

12 thin slices white bread
3 T. butter, softened
¼ c. chopped fresh watercress
1 (3 oz.) pkg. cream cheese
2 T. mayonnaise
¼ tsp. salt
¼ tsp. paprika
¼ tsp. curry powder
sprigs of fresh watercress or parsley

Remove crusts and flatten bread with rolling pin. Spread with butter. Combine remaining ingredients except sprigs in blender; spread on bread. Place small sprig of watercress on each end and roll up. Cut in half. Place on flat sheet and cover with damp towel. Refrigerate until ready to serve.

24 small sandwiches

CHINESE CHICKEN WINGS

Show ■
Go ■

1 c. water
1 c. soy sauce
1 c. brown or white sugar
¼ c. pineapple juice
¾ c. oil
1 tsp. ginger
1 tsp. garlic powder
20-24 chicken wings, cut in half

Mix all ingredients except chicken wings in a blender or food processor. Pour over chicken wings and marinate. When ready to bake wings, pour ½ cup of marinade on jelly roll pan, reserving the remaining marinade for basting the wings. Place the wings on top of the marinade. Bake at 350° for 45-60 minutes. Brush with reserved marinade. These freeze very well.

12-15 servings

OLD FASHIONED DEVILED EGGS

Show ■
Go ■

6 hard cooked eggs
2½ T. mayonnaise
1 T. prepared yellow mustard (or Dijon, if
    preferred)
2 tsp. white vinegar
½ tsp. salt
¼ tsp. pepper
paprika and/or minced fresh parsley for
    garnish

Peel and cut eggs in half. Mash the yolks with mayonnaise. Add the mustard, vinegar, salt and pepper. Taste and add more seasoings if needed. Mix well to desired consistency. Fill the whites and garnish each half with paprika and minced parsley.

12 servings

Finger lickin' good!

MANGO AVOCADO SALSA

Show ■
Go ■

2 fresh mangos, peeled, seeded and
   chopped
⅔ cup diced red bell pepper
2 T. chopped cilantro
⅓ c. minced red onion
2 T. white wine vinegar
1 T. sugar
½ tsp. salt
1 tsp. freshly ground black pepper
1 T. olive oil
1 avocado

In glass bowl, combine mangos, bell pepper, cilantro, red onion, vinegar, sugar, salt, pepper and olive oil. Chill 30 minutes. Just before serving, peel, seed and dice avocado and add to salsa mixture. Stir to blend and adjust seasoning to taste. Serve with chips or with grilled fish.

6 servings

LAYERED PESTO CHEESE SPREAD

Show ■
Go ☐

11 oz. cream cheese, softened
6 T. unsalted butter
⅔ c. grated parmesan cheese
1⅔ c. lightly packed fresh basil or parsley
   leaves, divided
3 T. olive oil
3 T. pine nuts, divided

Blend cream cheese and butter until well mixed. In a food processor or blender combine remaining ingredients, reserving 6 basil leaves and 6 to 8 pine nuts. Process until paste forms. Line small bowl with plastic wrap. Spread ⅓ of cream cheese mixture over bottom. Top with half of basil mixture. Repeat layers. Cover with remaining cheese mixture. Cover and chill for 2 hours. To serve, invert bowl onto serving plate and peel off plastic wrap. Garnish with reserved basil leaves and pine nuts. Serve with bread rounds or crackers. This may be made 2 days ahead.

10-12 servings

CHICKEN SATAY

Show ■
Go ■

4 chicken breasts, boned and skinned
½ c. peanut butter
½ c. vegetable oil
¼ c. white wine vinegar
¼ c. soy sauce
¼ c. lemon juice
4 whole garlic cloves, minced
8 sprigs parsley
2 tsp. crushed red pepper
2 tsp. fresh ginger, grated
8 small Bamboo skewers, soaked in water
    for 30 min

Warm peanut butter to liquefy. Blend all ingredients, except chicken, by hand or in a food processor. Reserve ¾ cup of peanut sauce for dipping. Cut chicken into cubes or strips; marinate 1 hour at room temperature or overnight in refrigerator. Remove chicken from marinade, thread onto skewers and barbeque or broil 10-15 min brushing frequently with marinade. Pass the skewers with reserved sauce for dipping.

Soups and Salads

THAT SOUP

Show ■
Go ■

1 (3½ -4 lb.) chicken, cut up
1 med. onion
2 carrots, sliced
1 parsnip, sliced
1 rib celery, sliced
1 T. salt
¼ tsp. white pepper
1 tsp. dill weed

Rinse chicken pieces well. Place in a 4-quart pot and cover with cold water. Bring to a boil and skim broth very well. Reduce to simmer and skim again. Add all remaining ingredients and cook until chicken is tender, 1-1½ hours. Remove chicken. Serve soup with the cooked vegetables and matzo balls.

3½ quarts

"EVERYONE CAN COOK" MATZO BALLS

Show ■
Go ■

2 rounded T. chicken fat
2 eggs, well beaten
2 tsp. chopped parsley
½ tsp. salt
pepper to taste
1 tsp. grated onion
⅔ tsp. baking powder
¾ c. matzo meal

Add chicken fat to eggs and mix in remaining ingredients. When well mixed, refrigerate for several hours. An hour before serving, shape loosely into small round balls and drop into rapidly boiling water for 15 minutes. Remove and add to hot soup.

20 matzo balls

"Everyone Can Cook" was the first Mount. Sinai Auxiliary Cookbook published in 1952

say ah-h!

CREAMED TOMATO BISQUE

Show ■
Go ■

½ c. butter
1 c. chopped celery
1 c. chopped onions
½ c. chopped carrots
⅓ c. flour
2 (28 oz.) cans tomatoes, drained and
    chopped
2 tsp. sugar
1 tsp. basil
1 tsp. marjoram
1 bay leaf
4 c. chicken broth
2 c. whipping cream
½ tsp. paprika
¼-½ tsp. curry powder
¼ tsp. white pepper
salt to taste

Melt butter and sauté celery, onion and carrots. Add flour and cook 2 minutes, stirring constantly. Add tomatoes, sugar, basil, marjoram, bay leaf and broth. Cover and simmer 30 minutes. Discard bay leaf. Purée one half at a time in blender. Add cream, paprika, curry, pepper and salt. Serve hot or cold. Freezes well.

6-8 servings

May add shrimp or crab to bisque and heat through.

ZUCCHINI SOUP

Show ■
Go □

1 med. onion, chopped
¼ c. butter
4 c. chicken stock
12 c. shredded zucchini
½ c. chopped parsley
¼ c. dill weed
¼ c. basil
1½ c. light cream or half cream and
    half buttermilk
salt and pepper to taste

Sauté onion in butter until golden. Add stock, zucchini and seasonings. Simmer about 25 minutes or until tender. Let cool. Place in food processor or blender and puree. Add cream, salt and pepper. Chill at least 4 hours.

12-14 servings

For the diet conscious, use all buttermilk. May also be served hot.

GAZPACHO

Show ■
Go ■

3 tomatoes, unpeeled and chopped
1 med. cucumber, unpeeled and chopped
1 med. onion, chopped
2 cloves garlic, crushed
1 (24 oz.) can tomato juice
⅓ c. wine vinegar
¼ c. olive oil
⅛ tsp. salt
¼ tsp. pepper
½ tsp. curry powder
1 c. mayonnaise

Blend tomatoes, cucumber, onion, garlic, 1 cup of tomato juice, vinegar and oil in food processor or blender. Add mixture to remaining tomato juice and season with salt and pepper. Chill overnight. Mix curry powder with mayonnaise. Serve gazpacho in individual bowls topped with a dollop of curried mayonnaise.

8-10 servings

ORIENTAL CELERY SOUP

Show ■
Go ■

sliced greens and tops of 1 celery stalk
2 qts. chicken broth
2 c. diagonally cut celery
2 c. sliced fresh mushrooms
½ tsp. ginger
½ tsp. garlic powder
1 tsp. soy sauce
½ c. sliced green onions
½ c. torn spinach

Simmer celery greens and tops in broth for 30 minutes; remove from broth. Add sliced celery, mushrooms, ginger, garlic powder and soy sauce. Simmer 7-10 minutes until celery is slightly tender. Add onions and spinach and simmer 1-2 minutes. Serve immediately.

6-8 servings

May add water chestnuts, cut-up chicken or shrimp.

CUCUMBER SOUP

Show ■
Go ■

3 med. cucumbers, peeled
1 med. leek
2 T. butter
2 bay leaves
1 T. flour
3 c. chicken broth
1 tsp. salt
1 c. whipping cream
juice of ½ lemon
dill weed to taste
dairy sour cream

Slice two cucumbers and the leek and sauté in butter. Add bay leaves and cook slowly until mixture is tender but not brown. Stir in flour, broth and salt; simmer 5 minutes. Remove bay leaves, press mixture through a sieve and chill. Remove seeds from third cucumber. Shred and add to chilled soup. Add cream, lemon juice and dill. Serve with a dollop of sour cream.

4 servings

Soup's on!

WATERCRESS SOUP

Show ■
Go □

3 T. butter
¼ c. minced onion
3 bunches fresh watercress, washed
   and stemmed
1½ c. water
1 tsp. salt
½ tsp. white pepper
2 T. flour
2 (13 oz.) cans chicken broth
2 c. milk
2 egg yolks
1 c. whipping cream

In a large saucepan, melt 1 tablespoon butter and sauté onion until golden. Add watercress, water, salt and pepper. Cook over high heat for 5 minutes. Pour small amount of mixture into food processor or blender and chop. Do not puree. Remove from processor. Repeat chopping process for remaining watercress mixture.

In a large saucepan, melt remaining butter, stir in flour, add chicken broth and milk. Bring to a boil. Discard half of liquid from watercress mixture. Add remaining watercress mixture to broth. Beat egg yolks and cream together. Stir 1 cup of the hot soup into the egg-cream mixture and add it to the soup, stirring constantly. Heat thoroughly. Do not boil.

8 servings

BEEF LENTIL SOUP

Show ■
Go ■

2 lbs. stewing beef
3 T. flour
2 tsp. salt
¼ tsp. pepper
3 T. oil
5 c. water
2 c. sliced celery
5 med. carrots, sliced
2 lg. onions, chopped
1 c. lentils
1 T. lemon juice
1 ½ tsp. salt
1 tsp. thyme

Cut beef into ½-inch cubes. Dredge in mixture of flour, 2 teaspoons salt and pepper. Heat oil in large pot and brown meat. Add water, cover and simmer 45 minutes. Add celery, carrots, onions, lentils, lemon juice, salt and thyme. Simmer covered, 1½ hours or until meat is tender. Stir occasionally. More water may be added if soup is too thick.

8 servings

SALAMI SOUP

Show ■
Go ■

2 (13 oz.) cans Crosse & Blackwell
   minestrone soup
1 (10½ oz.) can beef broth
1 (15 oz.) can tomato sauce with bits
1 (15 oz.) can water
salt to taste
¼ tsp. pepper
¼ tsp. thyme
3 med. carrots, sliced
1 c. chopped celery
1 (8 oz.) can kidney beans
1-2 lb. salami, cubed
1 c. shredded red cabbage
grated parmesan cheese

Place all ingredients except cabbage and cheese in large soup pot, cover and simmer for 2 hours on top of the stove or in the oven at 325°. Five minutes before serving, add cabbage. Garnish with parmesan cheese.

8 servings

May add 1 cup cooked pasta to soup

SNIDER'S RESTAURANT, BEMIDJI SHERRIED WILD RICE SOUP

Show ■
Go ■

⅔ c. wild rice
4½ c. chicken broth
1 T. minced onion
2 T. butter
¼ c. flour
5 c. chicken broth
¾ tsp. salt
1¼ c. cream
½ c. sherry
minced parsley or chives

Place wild rice in a strainer and rinse under tap water until water runs clear. In a large pot, bring broth to a boil, add rice and boil for 25-30 minutes. Stir occasionally. Drain and rinse in cold water. Set aside.

Sauté onion in butter until light brown. Blend in flour; add broth, stirring constantly, until thickened. Stir in wild rice and salt, simmer about 5 minutes. Blend in cream and sherry, and simmer until heated. Garnish with parsley or chives.

8 servings

BEAN AND BARLEY SOUP

Show ■
Go ■

¾ c. dried lima beans
½ c. barley
2 qts. water
1 lb. soup meat
1 soup bone
4-5 dried mushrooms (optional)
1 med. onion , diced
1 med. carrot, diced
1 tsp. salt
pepper to taste

Thoroughly wash beans and barley. Bring water to a boil in a 4-quart pot. Add meat, bone and beans. Boil a few minutes and skim. Add remaining ingredients, cover and simmer 2½ hours on top of stove or in oven at 325°. Add salt and pepper. Cut any meat off the bone and discard the bone. Soup will be thick, add water to thin.

6-8 servings

BEER CHEESE SOUP

Show ■
Go ■

¼ c. butter
½ c. shredded carrots
¼ c. chopped onion
4 c. whole milk
½ c. flour
2 c. chicken stock
1 T. chicken bouillon granules
2 c. well-packed shredded sharp
    cheddar cheese
1 tsp. Worcestershire sauce
2 dashes Tabasco sauce
salt and white pepper
1 (12 oz.) bottle strong beer or
    ale, room temperature
chopped green onions, Baco Bits
    and popcorn

Melt butter in a large saucepan. Add carrots and onion. Cook until onion is transparent but not brown. Transfer to blender or food processor. Add 3 cups of the milk and puree. Return to the pan. Add flour and blend well. Add remaining milk, chicken stock and bouillon. Cook over medium heat, stirring constantly, until it comes to a boil. Cook 2 minutes longer. Remove from heat, add cheese, Worcestershire sauce and Tabasco. Season with salt and pepper to taste. Just before serving, beat beer into soup with a wire whisk. Serve soup hot with side bowls of chopped green onion, Baco Bits and popcorn.

8-10 servings

COLD PLUM SOUP

Show ■
Go ■

1 (29 oz.) can purple plums, drained
    (reserving syrup), pitted and chopped
1 c. water
⅔ c. sugar
1 cinnamon stick
¼ tsp. white pepper
pinch of salt
½ c. whipping cream
½ c. dry red wine
1 T. cornstarch
2 T. lemon juice
1 tsp. grated lemon rind
1 c. dairy sour cream
3 T. brandy
dairy sour cream
cinnamon

In a saucepan, combine plums, reserved syrup, water, sugar, cinnamon stick, pepper and salt. Bring to a boil over moderately high heat. reduced heat to moderate and cook mixture, stirring occasionally, for 5 minutes. Stir in cream. Mix wine with cornstarch and add to soup mixture, stirring until thickened. Stir in lemon juice and rind, remove pan from heat. In a small bowl whisk the sour cream and brandy into ½ cup of soup. Add the mixture to the soup and stir until smooth. Let the soup cool; chill covered for at least 4 hours. Ladle into cups; garnish each serving with a dab of sour cream and sprinkle of cinnamon.

6-8 servings

BEEF VEGETABLE BARLEY SOUP

Show ☐
Go ■

1 lb. stew meat, cut up
2 marrow bones
½ c. pearl barley
1 onion, chopped
2 stalks celery, chopped
3 carrots, chopped
2 parsnips (optional), chopped
½ lb. fresh mushrooms, chopped
1 (8 oz.) frozen peas
1 (8 oz.) frozen corn
½ lb. fresh green beans or 1 c. frozen
    green beans
1 (8 oz.) lima beans (optional)
3 T. fresh parsley
1 T. dried dill weed
salt and pepper

In a large pot, place meat and bones. Cover with water by a few inches. Bring to a boil and skim. Add pearl barley. Simmer for one hour, and then add the rest of the ingredients. Cook until vegetables and meat are tender. Note: As it stands it will thicken. Add a small amount of water or broth and reheat.

6-8 servings

BLANCO CHICKEN CHILI

Show ■
Go ■

4 large boneless, skinless chicken breasts
2 bay leaves
½ c. white wine
2 med. onions, chopped
4-6 cloves garlic, minced
2 (4 oz) cans chopped green chiles
2 c. frozen corn
2 tsp. cumin
1 tsp. oregano
½ tsp. cayenne pepper
1-1½ c. grated Monterey Jack cheese
2 (15 oz.) cans white beans
2 (15 oz.) cans chicken broth
2 T. butter
2 T. olive oil
1 c. sour cream

Poach chicken breasts in boiling water with wine and bay leaves for approximately 10 minutes. Shred or cut chicken. Sauté garlic and onion in butter and olive oil. Add remaining ingredients, except cheese. Simmer 10 minutes. Add cheese. Serve with fresh cilantro and a dollop of sour cream.

6 servings

TORTILLA SOUP

Show ■
Go ■

2 T. olive oil
½ yellow onion, sliced thin
4 cloves garlic, chopped
¼ tsp. cumin
salt and freshly ground pepper
4 c. reduced sodium chicken broth
5 c. cooked chicken, shredded
1 (14½ oz) can fire roasted diced tomatoes,
    (i.e. Muir Glen Tomatoes)
2 T. fresh lime juice
¼ c. fresh cilantro
6 small corn tortillas, cut into ¼inch strips
½ ripe avocado, cubed
¼ c. shredded low-fat Monterey Jack
    cheese

In large stock pot, heat 1 T. olive oil. Add onions and sauté until soft, about 10 minutes. Add garlic, cumin, salt and pepper. Sauté 1 minute. Add chicken broth and bring to a simmer. Add chicken, tomatoes, lime juice and cilantro. Cover and remove from heat. Bake tortilla strips in 350° oven for 20-30 minutes until crisp. Ladle into bowls, top with avocado, cheese and tortilla strips.

4 servings

ROASTED ACORN SQUASH SOUP

Show ■
Go ☐

1 acorn squash
salt to taste
2 T. butter
¼ c. celery, chopped
¼ c. carrot, chopped
¼ c. yellow onion, chopped
2 c. chicken broth
¼ c. whipping cream
1½ tsp. fresh lemon juice
pepper to taste

Preheat oven to 300°. Cut squash in half and scrape out seeds and spongy membrane. Dislodge seeds from membrane, rinse thoroughly and set them aside. Place squash on jelly roll pan, cut side down. Bake for 1 hour and 15 minutes, until completely soft. In a medium saucepan melt butter. Add celery, carrot and onion, cooking gently for about 5 minutes. Add scraped flesh from cooked squash and chicken broth to mixture. Heat to boil. Immediately reduce heat and simmer for 25-30 minutes, until carrot and celery are tender. Puree soup mixture in food processor or blender. Return to saucepan and add cream, lemon juice, salt and pepper. Gently reheat. To prepare seeds, bake them at 300° for 25-35 minutes until crisp and golden. Sprinkle seeds with salt. Serve soup sprinkled with toasted squash seeds.

6 servings

CURRIED CHICKEN SALAD

Show ■
Go ☐

2 c. diced, cooked chicken, dark meat
1 apple, peeled and diced
1 c. diced fresh pineapple
¼ c. golden raisins
⅓ c. chopped dates
2 T. chopped chutney
1 c. shredded coconut
½ tsp. salt
1 T. curry powder
2 T. chicken consomme
1 c. mayonnaise (see index)
lettuce leaves

In a large bowl, combine chicken, apple, pineapple, raisins, dates, chutney, ½ cup coconut and salt. In small saucepan, mix curry powder and consomme. Simmer 2 minutes stirring into a smooth paste. Combine paste and mayonnaise. Stir into the salad ingredients. Arrange lettuce leaves on serving plates and pile the salad on the leaves. Sprinkle with remaining ½ cup coconut.

4 servings

OVERNIGHT CHICKEN SALAD

Show ■
Go ■

1 head iceberg lettuce, shredded
5 c. cooked white chicken, cut into chunks
salt and pepper to taste
pinch of sugar
6 hard-cooked eggs, sliced
1 (8 oz.) can sliced water chestnuts,
  drained
1 sweet red onion, sliced and separated
  into rings
1 c. chopped celery
1 (10 oz.) pkg. frozen peas, thawed
  (optional)
1 pt. mayonnaise
¼ c. Durkees Famous Sauce
1 (8 oz.) pkg. Swiss cheese slices
½ c. roasted almonds

Layer all ingredients in order listed, except mayonnaise, mustard, cheese and almonds in a 9x13-inch pan. Combine mayonnaise and mustard. Spread over salad to seal. Lay strips of cheese on top. Cover tightly with foil and refrigerate overnight. Just before serving, toss in a large bowl. Add more mayonnaise if necessary. Sprinkle with almonds.

8 servings

Curry powder, chutney and capers may be added to dressing.

CHUTNEY CHICKEN SALAD

Show ■
Go ■

3 lg. cooked chicken breasts
½ c. Oil and Vinegar Dressing (see index)
½ c. chutney
1 (8 oz.) can sliced water chestnuts
curry powder to taste
2 green onions, chopped
mayonnaise to moisten
½ c. pignoli (pine nuts)

Marinate chicken in dressing for a few hours. Cut into bite-size chunks. Add remaining ingredients. Sprinkle pignoli on top.

4-6 servings

May use 3 cups cooked shrimp or turkey in place of chicken.

FANTASTIC CHICKEN SALAD

Show ■
Go ☐

4 whole chicken breasts, boned
garlic powder
salt and pepper
2 T. oil
2 T. vinegar
2 T. orange juice
1 head romaine lettuce, chopped
1 head iceberg lettuce, chopped
1 bunch spinach, torn
1 (8 oz.) pkg. bean sprouts
4 oz. shredded Swiss cheese
¼ c. chopped fresh dill
3 avocados, peeled and quartered
1 (6 oz.) can pitted ripe olives, drained
1 (8 oz.) can sliced water chestnuts,
    drained
4 hard-cooked eggs, quartered
1 (2½ oz.) jar pimentos, sliced
1 red onion, sliced
fresh mushrooms (optional)

Dressing:
1 pt. mayonnaise
¼ c. chili sauce
¼ c. pickle relish
2 T. grated onion

Season chicken with garlic powder, salt and pepper. Bake at 350° until tender, about 30 minutes. Cut into large chunks. Marinate in oil, vinegar and orange juice for 24 hours. When ready to serve, combine remaining salad ingredients with chicken and mix well. For dressing, combine mayonnaise, chili sauce, pickle relish and grated onion. Toss with salad.

14 servings

You may add your favorite vegetables.

Lots of ingredients, but worth it!

THE NEW FRENCH CAFE
CHINESE CHICKEN SALAD

Show ■
Go ☐

Dressing:
8-10 cloves garlic, chopped fine
1 2-inch piece fresh ginger, chopped fine
1 c. tahini (sesame paste)
½ c. sugar
½ c. rice wine vinegar
½ c. sesame oil
1 c. Tamari soy sauce
1 T. red pepper flakes or cayenne
1-2 c. peanut oil

Salad ingredients:
napa cabbage
radishes, thinly sliced
carrots, thinly sliced
sprigs of fresh coriander
unsalted raw peanuts, roasted
chicken breasts, skinless, boneless;
    poached and julienned

For dressing, combine garlic, ginger, tahini, sugar, vinegar, oil, soy sauce and red pepper flakes. With wire whisk, (not in food processor) beat in peanut oil. For salad, cut chiffonades of cabbage (sliced across in rounds). Arrange on plate. Top with radishes, carrots, coriander, peanuts and chicken. Spoon dressing on top of salad.

3 pints dressing (20 servings)

Confucius say:
c'est magnifique!

LE PETIT CHEF
FRESH DUCK AND PEAR SALAD

Show ■
Go ☐

1 (4 lb.) duckling
3 ripe Bartlett pears, peeled and halved
7 oz. Mayonnaise (see index)
salt and pepper
12 Boston lettuce leaves
12 ripe olives
6 radishes
1 large tomato, cut in wedges
2 T. blanched whole almonds

Roast duckling until completely cooked. Cool. Remove skin and then meat from bones. Slice pears ⅛ inch thick. Make fresh mayonnaise. Toss sliced duckling and pears with mayonnaise. Add seasoning to taste. Serve on a bed of Boston lettuce with garnish of ripe olives, radishes and tomato wedges. Sprinkle almonds on top. Serve very cold.

6 servings

Elegant and impressive!

BROCCOLI SALAD

Show ■
Go ■

3 bunches raw broccoli
1 c. vinegar
1 T. sugar
1 T. dill weed
1 tsp. salt
1 tsp. pepper
1 tsp. garlic salt
1½ c. vegetable oil
lettuce leaves

Make flowerets of the broccoli. Mix remaining ingredients, except lettuce leaves and pour over the broccoli. Blend well. Cover and refrigerate for 24 hours. Drain and serve on lettuce leaves or as a relish.

8-10 servings

SNOW PEA SALAD

Show ■
Go ■

¼ c. red wine vinegar
¼ c. oil
2 tsp. Dijon mustard
1 tsp. crushed garlic
1 tsp. dried dill weed
salt and pepper to taste
1 c. half and half cream
6 artichoke hearts, canned or frozen
2 c. thinly sliced fresh mushrooms
1½ c. fresh snow peas, trimmed
    and halved
½ c. sliced toasted almonds

Combine vinegar, oil, mustard, garlic, dill weed, salt and pepper. Pour cream into mixture in a slow stream and whisk it to blend. Toss vegetables with dressing and garnish with almonds.

4-6 servings

ROMAINE-MUSHROOM SALAD

Show ■
Go ■

¼ c. tarragon wine vinegar
2 cloves garlic, crushed
¾ c. oil
1 T. minced parsley or 2 tsp. dill weed
1½ tsp. salt
¼ tsp. pepper
1 lb. fresh mushrooms, sliced
1 head romaine lettuce, cut up
¾ c. pitted ripe olives, drained
1 c. cherry tomatoes

In medium bowl, mix together vinegar, garlic, oil, parsley, salt and pepper. Add mushrooms to bowl and marinate for 1 hour. Add remaining vegetables. Toss and serve.

4-6 servings

MARINATED SALAD

Show ■
Go ☐

¾ c. sugar
½ c. oil
½ c. wine garlic vinegar
1 tsp. salt
½ tsp. pepper
dash red pepper
dash Tabasco
2 red or white onions, sliced
4 tomatoes, sliced
1 green pepper, sliced
2 radishes, sliced
2 avocados, sliced
2 cucumbers, sliced
1 (6 oz.) can ripe olives, sliced
1 med. head lettuce, sliced
croutons
2 hard-cooked eggs, sliced

Combine sugar, oil, vinegar, salt, pepper, red pepper and Tabasco to make marinade. Place onions, tomatoes, green pepper, radishes, avocados, cucumbers and ripe olives in a large bowl. Pour marinade over and mix well. Cover and refrigerate for 8 hours. One half hour before serving, add lettuce to vegetables; mix well. Top with croutons and eggs.

8-10 servings

CONFETTI SALAD

Show ■
Go ■

1 (17 oz.) can three bean salad, drained
1 (12 oz.) can whole kernel corn with red
    and green peppers, drained
2 green onions, thinly sliced or 2 slices
    red onion, separated
½ c. chopped celery
¼ c. vegetable or olive oil
¼ c. vinegar
1 T. sugar
½ tsp. salt (optional)
¼ tsp pepper

Combine three bean salad, corn, green onions and celery in medium size bowl. Combine remaining ingredients. Stir and pour over vegetables. Toss to coat well. Cover and chill for several hours or to quick-chill, place in freezer for 30 minutes. Keeps for several days in the refrigerator.

6 servings

CHEZ COLETTE SALADE NICOISE

Show ■
Go ☐

7 oz. fresh green beans
10 oz. potatoes
½ head Bibb lettuce
6 tomatoes, quartered
1 green pepper, cut in rings
4 ribs celery, chopped
½ cucumber, peeled and chopped
1 (7 oz.) can tuna, drained
3 hard-cooked eggs
1 (2 oz.) can anchovies, drained
1 (6 oz.) can ripe olives, drained
½ c. vinegar
¾ c. olive oil
salt and pepper

In small saucepan, cook beans in water until tender. Drain and cool. In large saucepan, cook potatoes in boiling salted water. Peel, cool and slice. Line sides of serving bowl with lettuce. Place sliced potatoes in the center and green beans around the potatoes. Arrange tomatoes on top of lettuce; then green pepper. Lay celery and cucumber on top. Place tuna in center of bowl. Cut eggs in half and arrange in bowl, cut side up. Decorate salad with anchovies and olives. For dressing, mix vinegar and olive oil; add salt and pepper to taste. Pour dressing over salad and serve.

4-6 servings

BLUE HORSE CAESAR SALAD

Show ■
Go ☐

1 head romaine lettuce
1 clove garlic, crushed
½ tsp. freshly ground pepper
juice of ½ lemon
1 tsp. Worcestershire sauce
1 (2 oz.) can anchovies, chopped
1 tsp. Dijon mustard
6 T. olive oil
2 T. red wine vinegar
2 coddled eggs (boiled 1 minute)
2 T. butter
½ c. croutons
½ c. freshly grated parmesan cheese

Trim romaine and cut lengthwise twice and then crisscross about 1½ inches apart. Reserve. Rub crushed garlic around the bottom of a large wooden bowl. Retain pulp. Add pepper, lemon juice, Worcestershire sauce and anchovies. With a fork, mash anchovies against bottom of the bowl into a fine paste. Add mustard, olive oil and vinegar. Blend thoroughly. In small bowl, beat coddled eggs. Add and mix vigorously until dressing begins to thicken. In a shallow pan, melt butter and sauté garlic pulp until it becomes aromatic. Add croutons and sauté until lightly browned. Place romaine in wooden bowl and toss thoroughly. Add ¼ cup parmesan cheese and croutons. Toss lightly. Serve salad on well chilled salad plates and top each portion with remaining parmesan cheese.

6 servings

It's show time...

CAESAR SALAD

Show ■
Go ■

1 clove garlic, crushed
1 tsp. Dijon mustard
1 tsp. anchovy paste
juice of ½ lemon
2 tsp. Worcestershire sauce
1 egg
salt to taste
1 lg. head romaine lettuce
4 T. melted butter
1 c. croutons
½ c. olive oil
⅙ c. red wine vinegar
¾ c. grated parmesan cheese
freshly ground pepper to taste

In a small bowl, mix together garlic, mustard, anchovy paste, lemon juice, Worcestershire sauce, egg and salt. Set aside. Separate lettuce leaves and wash. Dry with a paper towel. Tear the lettuce into pieces and place in a salad bowl. In pan of melted butter, lightly brown the croutons. Pour the mixture in the small bowl-and the olive oil and vinegar-over the lettuce, and toss lightly until mixed thoroughly. Add parmesan cheese. Toss just enough to mix the cheese, but not so the cheese becomes saturated. Add croutons, tossing once or twice. Top with freshly ground pepper and serve.

6 servings

UNPEELED POTATO SALAD

Show ■
Go ■

2½ lbs. sm. new red potatoes
8 hard-cooked eggs, cut in eighths
1-2 bunches green onions, chopped

Dressing:
¾ c. mayonnaise
¼ c. dairy sour cream
¼-½ c. Durkees Famous Sauce
1 T. dill weed
salt and pepper to taste

Wash and scrub new potatoes. Boil in large pot until tender. When potatoes are done, drain water and let cool. Cut unpeeled potatoes into cubes. Add eggs and onions. Mix with dressing and let marinate a few hours or overnight. For dressing, mix mayonnaise, sour cream, Durkees Sauce and dill weed. Season with salt and pepper.

8-10 servings

MARINATED SLICED TOMATOES

Show ■
Go ■

3 lg. tomatoes
⅓ c. olive oil
¼ c. red wine vinegar
1 tsp. salt
¼ tsp. pepper
½ clove garlic, crushed
2 T. finely chopped parsley
1 tsp. basil
2 T. finely chopped green onion
1 (4½ oz.) can sliced pitted ripe olives

Slice tomatoes ½ inch thick. Mix olive oil, vinegar, salt, pepper and garlic together, and pour evenly over tomatoes. Sprinkle with parsley, basil, onion and olives. Cover and refrigerate 1-3 hours before serving.

4-5 servings

MARINATED VEGETABLE SALAD

Show ■
Go ■

1½ c. sliced fresh mushrooms
1½ lbs. fresh or 2 (10 oz.) pkgs. frozen
   asparagus, cut in 2-inch pieces
1 (16 oz.) can garbanzos, drained
½ c. sliced ripe olives
½ c. sliced stuffed green olives
1 (9 oz.) pkg. frozen artichoke hearts,
   cooked
1 small onion, thinly sliced

Marinade:
1½ c. oil
½ c. red wine vinegar
3 T. light corn syrup
2 tsp. seasoned salt
1 tsp. basil
½ tsp. pepper

Place all salad ingredients in a large bowl. Mix marinade ingredients together in a 1 quart jar. Cover and shake well to blend. Pour marinade over salad and mix together. Cover and refrigerate overnight. When ready to serve, drain well.

8-10 servings

TORTELLINI SALAD

Show ■
Go ■

2 (15 oz.) pkgs. frozen meat tortellini
salt
drop of oil
5 green onions, chopped
1 (2½ oz.) jar pimentos, drained and
    julienned
2-3 knockwurst, boiled, skinned and
    diced
1 T. pignoli (pine nuts)

Dressing:
2 T. finely chopped dill
1 egg yolk
1 T. Dijon mustard
1 T. lemon juice
1 T. white wine or tarragon vinegar
2 T. dairy sour cream
1½ c. olive oil
salt and pepper to taste

Cook tortellini in salted boiling water with drop of oil for about 12 minutes; drain and cool thoroughly. For dressing, combine all ingredients. Toss with tortellini. Add remaining salad ingredients and serve chilled or at room temperature.

8-10 servings

Sure company pleaser!

DELI PASTA SALAD

Show ■
Go ■

1 (12 oz.) pkg. spiral pasta
1¼ c. ripe olives
1 c. chopped green pepper
¼ lb. hard salami, cut into thin strips
1 sm. red onion, cut into rings
¼-½ c. grated parmesan
¼ c. finely chopped parsley
1 (2 ½ oz.) jar pimento, drained
¾ c. Italian dressing

Cook pasta according to package directions. In large bowl, combine olives, green pepper, salami, onion, cheese, parsley, pimento and Italian dressing. Add pasta and toss well. Chill. Serve chilled or at room temperature. May be made the day before.

8-10 servings

Now, thatsa pasta!

TUNA SALAD

Show ■
Go ■

2 (7 oz.) cans white solid pack tuna, drained
1 (11 oz.) can mandarin oranges, drained
¼ lb. fresh mushrooms, sliced
4 oz. slivered almonds, toasted
1 c. small pimento-stuffed green olives,
    cut in half
1 c. water-packed artichokes, drained
1 c. sliced water chestnuts, drained
½ c. fried onion rings
½ c. sliced ripe olives

Dressing:
¼ c. mayonnaise
¼ c. sour cream
1 T. lemon juice
2 tsp. sugar
1 bunch green onions, sliced

Mix salad ingredients together in a large bowl. Combine dressing ingredients and mix with salad. Serve immediately.

8 servings

In tuna with the times

TARRAGON ORANGE SALAD

Show ■
Go ■

2 heads romaine lettuce
1 T. chopped parsley
2 green onions, sliced
1 (11 oz.) can mandarin oranges, drained
4 oz. slivered almonds
½ c. sugar

Dressing:
1 tsp. tarragon leaves
½ tsp. salt
⅛ tsp. pepper
3 tsp sugar
½ tsp. Dijon mustard
½ c. tarragon vinegar
1 c. oil

Break lettuce in pieces; place in large bowl. Add parsley, onions and mandarin oranges. Place almonds and sugar in small saucepan over low heat until sugar dissolves and coats almonds. Remove and spread on aluminum foil to cool. For dressing, place tarragon leaves, salt, pepper, sugar and mustard in mixing bowl or food processor. Beat in vinegar. Add oil slowly and mix until light and creamy. Refrigerate 20 minutes or more before serving. Toss salad and almonds with dressing.

8 servings

STRAWBERRY ROMAINE SALAD

Show ■
Go ■

Dressing:
1 c. mayonnaise
¼ c. vinegar
⅔ c. sugar
½ c. milk
2 T. poppy seeds
1 head romaine lettuce
1 pt. fresh strawberries, sliced
1 Spanish onion, sliced in rings
salt and pepper to taste

Mix mayonnaise, vinegar, sugar, milk and poppy seeds. Toss with romaine, strawberries and onion.

4 servings

TROPICAL FRUIT SALAD

Show ■
Go ☐

1 (20 oz.) can pineapple chunks
1 (11 oz.) can mandarin oranges
1 (8 oz.) can green grapes, drained
1-2 bananas, peeled and sliced
1 avocado, peeled and sliced
½ c. sugar
1 T. flour
1 egg, slightly beaten
¼ c. lemon juice

Drain and save the juice from the pineapple and oranges, separately. Combine drained fruits and add bananas and avocado. Prepare dressing by combining sugar, flour, egg, lemon juice and pineapple juice. If necessary, use reserved orange juice to make ¾ cup liquid. Mix well. Cook slowly, stirring constantly until thickened. Cool before mixing with salad fruits. Serve in lettuce-lined bowl.

6-8 servings

SUNSHINE MOLD

Show ■
Go ■

1 (6 oz.) pkg. lemon, lime or orange
    flavored gelatin
2 c. boiling water
1 (20 oz.) can crushed pineapple
1 (8 oz.) carton Cool Whip, thawed
1 (20 oz.) can lemon pie filling

Dissolve gelatin in boiling water. Drain pineapple; reserve juice. Add juice to gelatin; refrigerate for 2 hours. Beat gelatin in mixer for 1 minute. Fold in Cool Whip and pie filling at slow speed. Fold in pineapple. Pour into large lightly greased gelatin mold. Refrigerate until set. To serve, unmold and surround with fresh blueberries or strawberries.

8-10 servings

May make and serve in large ungreased compote.

CITRUS SALAD

Show ■
Go ■

5 oz. bag of mixed greens
1 (2¼ oz) can sliced black olives
1 (11oz.) can mandarin oranges
1 avocado, diced
mushroom slices (optional)
red onion slices (optional)

Brown sesame seeds in oven or on stove top. Add browned seeds to the rest of dressing ingredients. Shake well. Mix with salad greens, olives, oranges, avocado, mushroom slices and red onion

4 servings

Dressing
2 T. sesame seeds
⅓ c. canola or safflower oil
2 T. lemon juice
½ tsp. salt
1 tsp. onion powder
2 tsp. sugar

FARFALLE CHICKEN SALAD

Show ■
Go ■

1 lb. cooked diced chicken
1 lb. bowtie pasta (cooked and drained)
1 med. yellow onion, diced
2 stalks celery, diced small
1 lb. grapes, washed and sliced in half
1 c. toasted walnuts, whole

Combine the dry ingredients with the dressing. Refrigerate for 30 minutes before serving.

6 servings

Dressing
2 c. mayonnaise
½ c. honey
½ of a lemon, juiced
2 tsp. thyme, dried
¼ c. Dijon mustard
1 c. heavy cream
salt and pepper to taste

CASHEW CHICKEN SALAD

Show ■
Go ■

4-5 boneless chicken breasts, marinated in soy sauce (grilled and chilled)
1 c. hearts of celery, sliced thin
1 bunch green onions, chopped thin
1 (8 oz.) can honey roasted cashews
1 (2¼ oz.) can sliced black olives
2 cups red grapes, sliced in halves

Dressing:
Combine ⅔ c. mayonnaise and juice of one fresh lemon.

Toss all of the ingredients and mix with dressing. Refrigerate for 30 minutes before serving.

6 servings

FARMERS SALAD

Show ☐
Go ■

2 medium cucumbers, seeded and chopped into ½ inch pieces
1 large bunch radishes, thinly sliced
1 bunch green onions, including tops, chopped
1 (24 oz.) carton cottage cheese or
    1 (16 oz.) brick farmers cheese
1 c. sour cream
salt and pepper, to taste

Combine all ingredients thoroughly. Serve cold. You can also add seeded, chopped tomatoes and chopped dill pickles.

6-8 servings

BASIC VINAIGRETTE DRESSING

Show ■
Go ■

1 c. oil
¼ c. red or white wine vinegar
½ tsp. Dijon mustard
½ tsp. chopped parsley, tarragon or chives
salt
freshly ground pepper

Mix all ingredients until blended.

1¼ cups

RUBY RED DRESSING

Show ■
Go ■

1 c. sugar
1 c. lemon juice
1 c. oil
1 c. ketchup
1 c. chili sauce
¼ red onion, cut up
2 cloves garlic
1 tsp. Tabasco sauce
1 tsp. Worcestershire sauce

Combine all ingredients in blender or food processor.

1 quart

JUST PLAIN SALAD DRESSING

Show ■
Go ■

½ c. oil
½ c. brown sugar
½ c. granulated sugar
1 med. onion, peeled
⅓ c. ketchup
¼ c. cider vinegar
1 tsp. Worcestershire sauce

In blender or food processor, place all ingredients in order given. Blend well. Chill and serve over your favorite green salad.

1½ pints

BLEU CHEESE DRESSING

Show ■
Go ■

2 c. mayonnaise
½ c. dairy sour cream
¼ c. tarragon vinegar
4 tsp. sugar
½ tsp. dry mustard
1 sm. clove garlic, finely chopped
1 green onion, white part only,
    finely chopped
4 oz. bleu cheese, crumbled

Blend all ingredients, adding cheese last. Cover. Refrigerate at least 2 hours. Keeps well in refrigerator 2-3 weeks.

3 cups

POPPY SEED DRESSING

Show ■
Go ■

½ c. light corn syrup
1 tsp. dry mustard
1 tsp. salt
⅓ c. white vinegar
1 tsp. onion juice
dash Tabasco sauce
dash Worcestershire sauce
¼ tsp. chopped parsley
1 c. oil
½ T. poppy seeds

In blender or food processor, combine all ingredients except oil and poppy seeds. Gradually add oil until blended. Then add poppy seeds and blend again. Adjust seasonings to taste. Chill and serve. (A little sugar can be added for a sweeter dressing.)

1½ cups

SPINACH SALAD DRESSING

Show ■
Go ■

½ c. oil
1½ T. sugar
3 T. red wine vinegar
1 T. soy sauce
dash dry mustard

Combine all ingredients and mix well. Serve on your favorite spinach salad.

¾ cup

BLENDER CAESAR SALAD DRESSING

Show ■
Go ■

1 (2 oz.) can anchovies, drained
⅔ c. oil
3¾ T. lemon juice
1 tsp. Worcestershire sauce
1 tsp. Dijon mustard
ground pepper

Combine all ingredients in blender.

1 cup

Great with romaine lettuce, croutons and parmesan cheese.

QUICK SALAD DRESSING OR MARINADE

Show ■
Go ■

⅓ c. tarragon vinegar
½ c. oil
2 tsp. salt
½ tsp. cracked pepper
2 cloves garlic, minced
1 tsp. chopped parsley (optional)

Mix in jar and refrigerate. Shake well before using.

¾ cup

Excellent marinade for mushrooms, onions, zucchini, carrots and celery, or as a regular salad dressing on greens.

SEAFOOD DRESSING

Show ■
Go ■

1 (7 ½ oz.) can king crabmeat, shredded
⅓ c. mayonnaise
⅓ c. dairy sour cream
⅓ c. chili sauce

Combine ingredients in medium bowl. Cover and chill.

2 cups

Great with Egg Salad Mold (see index) or lettuce salad.

CHEZ COLETTE HOUSE DRESSING

Show ■
Go ■

3 T. mayonnaise
1 T. Dijon mustard
1 T. yellow mustard
3 T. red wine vinegar
1 tsp. salt
½ tsp. freshly ground pepper
½ tsp. tarragon
2 c. oil

Mix mayonnaise with mustards, vinegar and seasonings until smooth. Add the oil slowly. Adjust seasonings to taste. Add more oil if dressing is too thick.

2½ cups

This one's on the house!

Breads

WHOLE WHEAT CHALLAH

Show ■
Go ☐

2 pkgs. active dry yeast
½ c. warm water
pinch of sugar
6 c. unbleached flour
2 c. whole wheat flour
1½ c. warm water
4 eggs, beaten
¾ c. safflower oil
1½ T. salt
¾ c. sugar or ¼ c. sugar plus ¼ c. honey
1 egg, beaten with 1 T. water
poppy or sesame seeds

Mix together yeast, ½ cup water and pinch of sugar. Set aside until dissolved and puffy. In a large bowl, mix together flours, 1½ cups water, eggs, oil, salt and sugar with hands or wooden spoon. Blend in yeast mixture. Batter will be a bit sticky. Cover bowl with warm dampened towel and set in warm place to rise.

When dough has doubled its original size, punch down and knead for 2 minutes. Cover and let rise again. After second rising, place dough on a floured surface. Divide into 2 sections. Divide each section into 3 long rolls and braid into 2 loaves. Put each loaf in a greased 5x9-inch loaf pan or on large greased cookie sheet. Let stand 20-30 minutes. Bake at 350° for 15 minutes. Lightly brush tops with poppy or sesame seeds. Lower oven temperature to 325° and continue baking for 30 minutes until brown. Remove and cool on racks. Freezes well; serve warm by reheating at 350° for 10-15 minutes wrapped in foil.

2 loaves

HONEY CHALLAH

Show ■
Go ☐

2 pkgs. active dry yeast
4 tsp. salt
¾ c. honey
1¾ c. warm water
2 c. flour
1 c. oil
3 eggs
6- 6½ c. flour
1 egg, beaten
sesame seeds

Mix yeast, salt, honey and water in large bowl. Let stand for 5 minutes. Add 2 cups flour and beat well. Blend in oil, eggs and remaining flour. Turn onto lightly floured board and knead. Place back in bowl, cover and let rise in a warm place until doubled in size, about 2-3 hours. Punch down; divide into 3 sections. Divide each section into 3 long rolls and braid into loaves. Place on cookie sheets. Cover; let rise 45 minutes. Brush with egg and sprinkle with sesame seeds. Bake at 325° for 40-45 minutes.

3 small loaves

OATMEAL BREAD

Show ■
Go ☐

2 pkgs. active dry yeast
1 T. sugar
½ c. warm water
½ c. shortening
2 c. boiling water
1½ c. quick oatmeal
¾ c. molasses
½ c. brown sugar
¼ c. sugar
1½ tsp. salt
3 eggs, beaten
9-9½ c. flour
raisins, plumped in hot water (optional)

Dissolve yeast and 1 tablespoon sugar in water; let rise about 10 minutes. Meanwhile, mix together remaining ingredients except flour; cool to lukewarm. Mix part of flour in and add the yeast mixture. Add balance of flour by mixing and kneading until smooth. Raisins may be added. Let rise in a covered bowl until doubled. Shape into three loaves and place in greased 5x9-inch pans. Let rise again. Bake at 375° for 45 minutes.

3 loaves

BUTTERMILK GRAHAM BREAD

Show ■
Go ■

3 c. graham whole wheat flour
2 c. unbleached flour
1 tsp. salt
2 tsp. baking soda
1 tsp. baking powder
½ c. brown sugar
2½ c. plus 2 T. buttermilk
½ c. molasses
1 c. raisins or currants, plumped
    in hot water

Mix dry ingredients together. Blend in liquids until moistened. Stir in raisins and pour into 2 greased 5x9-inch loaf pans. Bake at 350° for 1 hour.

2 loaves

BEER BREAD

Show ■
Go ■

1 (12 oz.) can beer, room temperature
3½ c. self-rising flour
3 T. sugar

In mixing bowl, combine all ingredients by hand. Pour batter into four 3¼x5¾-inch loaf pans. Bake at 350° for 1 hour.

4 mini loaves

EXTRA TERRIFIC BREAD LOAF

Show ■
Go ■

1 loaf French bread
1 c. butter, softened
¾ T. dry mustard
2 T. poppy seed
2½ T. finely chopped green onion
1 (8 oz.) pkg. Swiss cheese, cut diagonally
    to form triangles
1 med. onion, thinly sliced

Remove side crust from bread. Slice 16 pieces ¾ way through to bottom crust. Mix together butter, mustard, poppy seed and green onion. Blend well. Spread mixture between slices, saving some for top and sides of loaf. Place 1 cheese triangle and 1 onion ring in each slit between pieces. Spread top and sides with remaining butter. Wrap in foil. Heat at 325° for 20-30 minutes or until cheese has melted. Open foil last 10 minutes to brown.

16 servings

POPPY SEED BREAD

Show ■
Go ■

2½ c. sugar
2½ c. oil
2 c. evaporated milk
5 eggs
½ c. milk
5 c. flour
4½ tsp. baking powder
¼ tsp. salt
½ c. poppy seeds
2½ tsp. vanilla

In electric mixer bowl, combine sugar, oil, evaporated milk, eggs and milk; beat at medium speed. Mix well. Sift together flour, baking powder and salt; slowly blend into creamed mixture. Add poppy seeds and vanilla; mix until smooth. Pour batter into two generously-greased 5x9-inch loaf pans. Bake at 350° for 55 minutes, until golden brown.

2 loaves

A sweet quick bread that may be baked as muffins; reduce baking time to 30 minutes.

CARROT COCONUT BREAD

Show ■
Go ■

3 eggs
½ c. oil
1 tsp. orange or lemon extract
2 c. finely shredded carrots
2 c. shredded coconut
1 c. raisins
1 c. chopped pecans
2 c. flour
½ tsp. salt
1 tsp. baking soda
1 tsp. baking powder
1 tsp. cinnamon
1 c. sugar

In large bowl, beat eggs until light. Stir in oil and extract. Add carrots, coconut, raisins and nuts. Mix well. Combine flour, salt, baking soda, baking powder, cinnamon and sugar. Stir into first mixture until blended. Spoon mixture into a greased and floured 5x9-inch loaf pan. Bake at 350° for 1 hour or until browned. Remove from pan and cool. Wrap in foil and refrigerate overnight. May be frozen.

1 loaf

ZUCCHINI NUT BREAD

Show ■
Go ■

3 c. flour
2 tsp. cinnamon
1 tsp. baking soda
1 tsp. salt
¾ tsp. baking powder
1 T. grated lemon rind
2 c. grated, unpeeled zucchini
1 c. chopped walnuts
1¾ c. sugar
1 c. oil
4 eggs
⅛ tsp. lemon juice

Blend together flour, cinnamon, baking soda, salt and baking powder. Set aside. In medium bowl, combine lemon rind, zucchini and walnuts; set aside. In large mixing bowl, combine sugar, oil, eggs and lemon juice; beat until smooth. Add dry ingredients and mix well. Stir in zucchini mixture and combine. Divide batter evenly between two greased and floured 5x9-inch loaf pans. Bake at 350° for 55-60 minutes or until cake tester comes out clean. Cool in pan 10 minutes; remove and cool completely. Cut in thin slices.

2 loaves

STRAWBERRY BREAD

Show ■
Go ■

3 c. flour
1 tsp. baking powder
1 tsp. baking soda
1 tsp. salt
2 tsp. cinnamon
2 c. sugar
4 eggs, well beaten
1¼ c. oil
2 (10 oz.) pkgs. frozen strawberries, thawed
1¼ c. chopped pecans
¼ c. strawberry jam

Mix together flour, baking powder, baking soda, salt, cinnamon and sugar. Add eggs, oil, strawberries, pecans and jam. Blend. Pour batter into 2 well-greased 5x9-inch loaf pans. Bake at 350° for 1 hour.

2 loaves

BANANA CHOCOLATE CHIP LOAF

Show ■
Go ■

3 ripe bananas
½ c. butter or margarine, melted
1 c. sugar
2 eggs
1 tsp. vanilla
2 c. flour
1 tsp. baking soda
¼ tsp. salt
¾ c. chocolate chips
powdered sugar

In food processor or blender, combine bananas, butter, sugar, eggs and vanilla. Blend well. Add flour, soda and salt. Fold in chocolate chips. Pour batter into a greased 5x9-inch loaf pan. Bake at 350° for 1 hour. Cool and remove from pan. Sprinkle with powdered sugar. Wrap tightly in foil. This loaf is better the second day. Freezes well.

1 loaf

HEALTH NUT BANANA BREAD

Show ☐
Go ■

½ c. chopped walnuts
2 c. flour
1 tsp. baking powder
1 tsp. baking soda
½ c. corn oil margarine
½ c. sugar
1 c. mashed banana (3 sm. or 2 med.)
3 T. skim milk
1 tsp. vanilla
½ c. golden raisins or chopped dates

Toast walnuts in 350° oven for 10 minutes. Blend together flour, baking powder and baking soda; set aside. Cream margarine and sugar. Add bananas, milk and vanilla. Mix well. Blend in dry ingredients. Stir in nuts and raisins. Pour batter into a greased 5x9-inch loaf pan. Bake at 350° for 55 minutes or until top is golden brown and firm.

1 loaf

This is an egg-less banana bread

A top banana!

CRANBERRY ORANGE BREAD

Show ■
Go ■

2 c. flour
1 c. sugar
1½ tsp. baking powder
½ tsp. salt
½ tsp. baking soda
2 T. butter, softened
¾ c. orange juice
1 egg
1 c. raw cranberries, cut in half
½ c. chopped nuts (optional)

In large bowl place dry ingredients. Add butter, juice and egg; mix well. Fold in cranberries and nuts. Pour into greased 5x9-inch loaf pan. Bake at 350° for 50 minutes. Cool 5 minutes and remove from pan.

1 loaf

MACADAMIA NUT LOAF

Show ■
Go ■

1 c. unsalted butter, softened
2 c. sugar
4 eggs
1 c. mashed banana
4 c. flour
2 tsp. baking powder
1 tsp. baking soda
½ tsp. salt
1 (15½ oz.) can crushed pineapple,
    undrained
1 c. shredded coconut
1 c. chopped macadamia nuts

Beat butter and sugar together thoroughly. Add eggs and mix well. Stir in bananas. Add flour, baking powder, baking soda and salt to creamed mixture. Fold in pineapple, coconut and nuts. Pour into 2 greased 5x9-inch loaf pans. Bake at 350° for 65-70 minutes.

2 loaves

APRICOT NUT BREAD

Show ■
Go ■

8 oz. chopped dates
1½ c. chopped dried apricots
2 tsp. baking soda
1½ c. sugar
8 T. butter
1¾ c. apricot nectar, boiling
2 eggs, slightly beaten
2½ c. flour
1 c. chopped nuts

In large bowl, combine dates, apricots, soda, sugar and butter. Cover with boiling apricot nectar. When cool, add eggs, flour and nuts. Mix well. Pour into two greased 8x4-inch loaf pans. Bake at 350° for 55-60 minutes.

2 loaves

HEALTHY MUFFINS

Show ■
Go ■

1-15 oz. box raisin bran
½ c. raisins or chopped dates
3 c. natural sugar
5 c. flour
1 tsp. salt
2 T. baking soda
4 eggs, beaten
1 qt. buttermilk
1 c. oil
2 T. vanilla
¾ c. unprocessed bran
½ c. wheat germ

In large bowl mix together raisin bran, raisins or dates, sugar, flour, salt, soda, eggs, buttermilk, oil and vanilla. Gently stir in the bran and wheat germ. Do not over stir. Spoon into greased muffin tins. Bake at 400° for 15-20 minutes

Tons of muffins

For miniature muffin tins bake only 10-15 minutes. Batter keeps up to 6 weeks in refrigerator.

"Take two and call me in the morning"

SWEDISH KRINGLE

Show ■
Go ■

Dough:
½ c. butter
1 c. flour
1 T. water

Filling:
½ c. butter
1 c. water
1 c. flour
3 eggs
½ tsp. almond extract

Icing:
2 c. powdered sugar
milk
½ tsp. almond extract

sliced almonds

Combine ½ cup butter, 1 cup flour and 1 tablespoon water. Mix to consistency of pie crust; pat into 2 oblong shapes about 4 inches wide on a lightly greased cookie sheet. Bring to a boil ½ cup butter, 1 cup water and quickly stir in 1 cup flour and the eggs, one at a time. Add ½ teaspoon almond extract. Spread mixture over dough on cookie sheet. Bake at 375° for 45 minutes. Remove from oven and cool. For icing, add enough milk to powdered sugar until it is of spreading consistency; add ½ teaspoon almond extract. Spread on kringles. Sprinkle top with almonds; slice and serve.

2 kringles

BLUEBERRY COFFEE CAKE

Show ■
Go ■

¼ c. butter
¾ c. sugar
1 egg
2 c. flour
2 tsp. baking powder
½ tsp salt
½ c. milk
1 pt. blueberries, washed, drained and
    lightly dusted with flour

Streusel:
¼ c. flour
¼ c. sugar
2 T. butter

Cream ¼ c. butter and ¾ cup sugar. Add egg. Sift together 2 cups flour, baking powder and salt. Add dry ingredients to creamed mixture alternately with milk. Fold in blueberries. Pour batter into a greased 5x9-inch loaf pan. Combine ¼ cup flour, ¼ cup sugar and 2 tablespoons butter until crumbly, and sprinkle over batter. Bake at 350° for 1 hour.

1 loaf

CHOCOLATE CHIP COFFEE CAKE

Show ■
Go ■

½ c. butter, softened
1 c. sugar
½ tsp. salt
2 eggs, slightly beaten
2 c. flour
1 tsp. baking powder
1 tsp. baking soda
1 c. dairy sour cream
1 tsp. vanilla

Streusel:
½ c. sugar
1 tsp. cinnamon
¾ c. chocolate chips
½ c. brown sugar
½ c. chopped nuts (optional)

In mixer bowl, cream butter and sugar. Add salt, eggs and mix well. Sift together flour, baking powder and baking soda. Add to creamed mixture alternately with the sour cream. Add vanilla.

For streusel, combine sugar, cinnamon, chocolate chips, brown sugar and nuts. Spread half of the cake batter in a greased 9x9-inch pan. Sprinkle with half of streusel mixture. Spread remaining cake batter on top and sprinkle with remaining streusel mixture. Bake at 350° for 35-40 minutes. When toothpick comes out clean, cake is done.

As a variation, a 10-inch tube pan can be used. Cool upright for 15 minutes, invert to remove and turn streusel side up on serving platter.

16-20 pieces

good morning, Mr. Chips!

MARBLEIZED COFFEE CAKE

Show ■
Go ■

4 eggs, well beaten
¾ c. oil
¾ c. water
1 tsp. vanilla
1 T. butter extract
1 (1.4 oz.) envelope whipped
    topping mix
1 (3⅝ oz.) pkg. instant vanilla
    pudding mix
1 (#2 Deluxe) Duncan Hines
    yellow cake mix

Streusel:
¼ c. sugar
2 tsp. cinnamon
¼ c. chopped pecans

Glaze:
¾ c. powdered sugar, sifted
1½ T. milk
1 tsp. vanilla
1 tsp. butter extract

chopped pecans

Combine eggs, oil, water, vanilla and butter extract in large mixing bowl. Add whipped topping mix, pudding mix and cake mix. Beat 7 minutes. Grease a 15x4x4-inch or two 9x5-inch loaf pans and pour in ¾ of batter.

For streusel, combine sugar, cinnamon and pecans; sprinkle on top of batter in pan. Pour remaining batter over streusel mixture. With a knife, swirl through batter to marbleize. Bake at 350° for 50-60 minutes. Cake is done when toothpick inserted in center comes out clean. Let cool before removing from pan. For glaze, combine sugar, milk vanilla and butter extract. Pour glaze over cake and sprinkle with pecans.

24 slices

place in the oven and see what develops

CARAMEL PECAN ROLLS

Show ■
Go □

1 cake yeast
½ c. warm water
1 c. milk
½ c. sugar
1 tsp. salt
2 eggs, slightly beaten
1 c. butter
4 c. flour
1 c. butter
1 c. brown sugar
1 tsp. cinnamon

Syrup:
1½ c. brown sugar
1½ c. butter
4½ T. honey

2 (8 oz.) pkgs. whole pecans

Dissolve yeast in warm water. Scald milk; add sugar and salt. Cool to lukewarm. Add eggs to milk mixture and combine with yeast. In separate bowl, cut 1 cup butter into flour until pea size. Add one-half of yeast mixture. Mix well. Add remaining mixture and blend. Cover and refrigerate overnight.

Next day, separate dough into two pieces. Roll 1 piece into 11x18-inch rectangle. Melt 1 cup butter and brush surface generously then sprinkle with mixture of brown sugar and cinnamon. Roll up jelly roll fashion, tightly sealing edges, and cut into 18 pieces. Repeat for second piece.

To make syrup, mix brown sugar, butter and honey together; boil 2 minutes. Preheat oven to 180°. Pour syrup evenly into ungreased muffin tins. Place 3 or 4 pecan halves on top of syrup and place roll in tin cut side up. Cover with clean dish towels. Turn off oven. Place the tins on cookie sheets in oven for 30 minutes; remove.

Re-heat oven to 375°; remove towels and bake rolls 25-35 minutes. Remove from oven and place a cookie sheet over tins and turn upside down. Do not take the tins off the rolls for 1 minute. Tap gently and remove tins. Let cool.

36 rolls

PETITE CARAMEL ROLLS

Show ■
Go ■

2 c. butter or margarine, softened
1 (16 oz.) sm. curd cottage cheese
3½ c. flour
½ c. sugar plus 1 tsp. cinnamon
½ c. butter, melted
½ c. brown sugar
¼ c. chopped pecans

Blend together butter, cottage cheese and flour to form a smooth dough. Divide into 4 parts. Wrap each ball separately in floured waxed paper. Refrigerate a few hours or overnight. Roll one ball at a time to about a 5x10-inch rectangle, ⅛ inch thick. Sprinkle with cinnamon-sugar mixture and roll up dough starting with long side. Place ½ teaspoon butter, ½ teaspoon brown sugar and ¼ teaspoon pecans in bottom of each small muffin cup. Cut dough into 1 inch slices and place in muffin cup cut-side up. Bake at 375° for 35-40 minutes or until brown.

4 dozen

NEW ENGLAND BRAN MUFFINS

Show ■
Go ■

1 c. pure bran
1 c. water
1 c. flour
¼ c. brown sugar
½ tsp. salt
½ tsp. baking powder
1 egg
3 T. honey
¼ c. oil
½ c. chopped dates
½ c. chopped nuts (optional)

Soak bran in water. Mix together flour, sugar, salt, baking soda and baking powder. Add egg, honey, oil and bran. Stir only to moisten. Add dates and nuts. Spoon into greased muffin tins. Bake at 400° for 20 minutes.

12 muffins

May use half whole wheat flour.

PERFECT POPOVERS

Show ■
Go ■

6 eggs
½ c. milk
½ c. water
¼ c. oil
1 c. flour
½ tsp. salt
grated parmesan cheese (optional)

Beat eggs, milk, water and oil by hand or slow speed on mixer. Add flour and salt. Mix at medium speed until smooth. Preheat oven to 450°. Heat popover pans or individual custard cups on cookie sheet for 15 minutes. Remove from oven and coat with oil. Dust the pans with parmesan cheese, if desired. Fill each cup ½ to ¾ full. Bake at 450° for 30 minutes. Reduce heat to 300° and bake 15 minutes more.

10 popovers

POPPY SEED SCONES

Show ■
Go ■

½ c. butter
2 T. sugar
2 eggs, beaten
¾ c. dairy sour cream
2 c. flour
1 T. baking powder
1 T. poppy seeds

Using pastry blender, cut butter into sugar until crumbly. Mix eggs and sour cream and add to mixture. Add flour, baking powder and poppy seeds; mix well. Place on floured board, roll into 12 inch circle and cut into 12 wedges. Place on greased cookie sheet. Bake at 450° for 15 minutes.

12 scones

BRIOCHE

Show ■
Go ☐

⅓ c. warm water
1 pkg. active dry yeast
1½ T. sugar
¼ tsp. salt
⅔ c. butter, softened
4 lg. eggs
3 c. flour
1 egg yolk
2 tsp. water

The night before, place water in a large electric mixer bowl and sprinkle with yeast. Add sugar and salt; stir. Beat in butter, eggs and 2 cups flour for 4 minutes on medium speed. Add remaining 1 cup flour and beat at low speed for 1 minute. Cover with buttered waxed paper and damp towel. Let rise in warm place until doubled, about 2½ hours. Punch down; cover bowl again with buttered waxed paper and damp towel. Refrigerate overnight.

The next day, grease a 5 cup brioche mold with shortening, not butter. Pinch off ⅙ of dough and roll into a small ball. Knead rest of dough for 1 minute until smooth. Form an oval shape and place in brioche mold. Make an indentation in center of dough and insert rolled ball. Cover and let rise until doubled, about 2 hours. Mix together egg yolk and water. Brush top. Cover loosely with foil and bake at 375° for 20 minutes. Remove foil and bake 30-40 minutes longer or until golden brown. Watch carefully. To test, tap top of bread; if it sounds hollow it's done. Remove from oven and let cool for 20 minutes in pan.

1 large bread

This can also be baked in a greased 2 lb. coffee can

Voila'!

CINNAMON BUTTERHORNS

Show ■
Go ☐

1½ c. scalded milk
½ c. butter
3 eggs
½ c. sugar
½ tsp. salt
1 pkg. yeast
¼ c. warm water, 105°-115°
6 c. all-purpose flour

Filling:
½ c. softened butter
1 c. sugar
1 T. cinnamon

Glaze:
1 egg
2 T. milk
pearl sugar or crushed sugar cubes

In a large bowl, combine milk and butter; stir until butter is melted. Beat in eggs, sugar and salt. In a small dish, dissolve the yeast in the warm water; let stand 5 minutes. Add to cooled milk mixture. Stir in flour, beating to make a smooth but thick batter. Cover and refrigerate 2 to 24 hours.

Divide dough into 4 parts. On floured surface roll each part out to make a 12 inch circle. Spread with softened butter. Mix cinnamon and sugar together and sprinkle over the dough evenly. Cut each circle into 8 wedges. Roll up each wedge, starting from the wide end, to make a crescent-shaped roll. Cover baking sheets with parchment paper or lightly grease them. Place rolls on the prepared baking sheets. Let rise about 45 minutes until puffy.

Beat the egg and milk together and brush rolls lightly with the mixture. Sprinkle with sugar. Preheat oven to 375°. Bake 13-15 minutes until golden.

Makes 32 rolls.

BREAD MACHINE CHALLAH

Show ■
Go ■

2 eggs
½ c. oil
1 c. water
½ c. honey
½ tsp. salt
4 c. bread flour
2 tsp. yeast
1 egg, beaten with 1 T. water
poppy or sesame seeds (optional)

Place all liquid ingredients first into bread pan. Then add all dry ingredients with yeast on top. Set machine on "dough" setting. When cycle is complete, remove dough. Knead and braid dough. Let rise 45 minutes. Brush with egg–water mixture, sprinkle with poppy seeds or sesame seeds as desired. Bake 35 minutes at 350°.

Makes one 2 lb. loaf.

CINNAMON STREUSEL BANANA BREAD

Show ■
Go ■

1 c. butter, softened
2 c. sugar
2 eggs
4 ripe bananas
1 c. sour cream
2 tsp. baking soda
3 c. flour
⅛ tsp. salt
2 tsp. baking powder
1 tsp vanilla

Topping
⅓ c. brown sugar
1-2 tsp. cinnamon

Preheat oven to 350°. Grease two 5x9 inch loaf pans. Cream butter and sugar. Add eggs and cream again. Add bananas and mix well. Add baking soda to sour cream and mix. (Use a 2 cup container because the sour cream will rise). Sift together flour, baking powder and salt. Add flour mixture to butter mixture alternately with sour cream, beginning and ending with the dry ingredients. Stir in vanilla. Spread half the batter into the prepared pans. Sprinkle with half the topping mixture. Spread other half of batter on top and sprinkle with remaining topping. Swirl a knife through the batter. Bake about 50-60 minutes or until cake tests done using a toothpick. Reverse onto a cake rack until cool.

Makes two loaves.

Entrees

IN-THE-OVEN ITALIAN STEW

Show ■
Go ■

2 lbs. chuck roast, cubed
2 onions, quartered
4 potatoes, peeled and quartered
2 carrots, peeled and quartered
¼ c. dry Italian flavored bread crumbs
½ tsp. salt
1 T. basil
1 T. oregano
1 tsp. thyme
1 (16 oz.) can tomatoes with juice
¾ c. dry red wine
1 tsp. Worcestershire sauce
½ (10 oz.) pkg. frozen baby peas, thawed
½ lb. fresh mushrooms, sliced

In a large casserole, combine all ingredients except peas and mushrooms. Cover and bake at 325° for 3 hours. Add remaining vegetables and bake uncovered for another 30-40 minutes.

4-6 servings

May omit potatoes and serve over buttered noodles or rice.

BARBECUED BRISKET

Show ■
Go ■

1 (5-7 lb.) beef brisket
3 cloves garlic, slivered
pepper and paprika to taste
1 c. honey
1½-2 c. ketchup
1 envelope dry onion
3-5 drops liquid smoke
1 T. soy sauce

Make slits on top of brisket, insert garlic slivers and place in large roasting pan. Season with pepper and paprika. Combine honey, ketchup, onion soup, liquid smoke and soy sauce; cook over low heat until blended. Pour sauce over brisket. Seal pan with foil and bake at 325° for 4 hours. Remove foil last 30 minutes to brown.

16-18 servings

SWEET AND SOUR BRISKET

Show ■
Go ■

1 (5½ lb.) beef brisket
Lawry's seasoned salt
onion salt
pepper
garlic powder
1 qt. sauerkraut, drained
1½ c. brown sugar
3 c. tomato juice
¾ c. ketchup

Season brisket with salts, pepper and garlic powder. Place in roasting pan and surround with sauerkraut. Top with brown sugar and tomato juice. Bake covered at 325° for 3 hours. Add ketchup and uncover last 30 minutes.

6-8 servings

CHILI CON CARNE

Show □
Go ■

2 lbs. ground beef
1 med. onion, chopped
2 cloves garlic, crushed
1 (15 oz.) can tomato sauce
1 (12 oz.) can tomato paste
1 (12 oz.) can water
2 tsp .salt
¼ tsp. freshly ground pepper
¾ tsp. ground cumin
3-4 T. chili powder
dash Tabasco
2 (15½ oz.) cans kidney beans

Brown beef, onion and garlic. Drain off excess fat. Stir in remaining ingredients except beans. Simmer 30-45 minutes. Stir in beans and heat another 10 minutes. Adjust seasoning. Cool and refrigerate. Reheat next day.

6 servings

Best made day before. Tabasco gets hotter as it blends with chili so start out with a dash and add more if needed.

For a "chili" day... Brrr

CHICAGO STYLE PIZZAS

Show ■
Go ☐

Filling (prepare night before):
2 lbs. ground beef
2 cloves garlic, crushed
1 tsp. oregano
1 tsp. basil
pinch of sugar
¼ tsp. fennel seed

Dough:
2 pkgs. active dry yeast
¾ tsp. sugar
¼ c. water
4 c. flour
¼ c. oil
½ tsp salt
9 oz. beer, room temperature

Topping:
salt
1 c. grated parmesan cheese
2 lbs. mozzarella cheese
2 (28 oz.) cans whole tomatoes, drained
    and coarsely chopped
oregano
basil
salt
pepper
grated parmesan cheese

In a large bowl, mix together all filling ingredients. Cover tightly and refrigerate. For dough, combine yeast, sugar and water in a small bowl. Stir and let set until it doubles in size, about 10 minutes. In a large bowl, combine the yeast mixture with the flour, oil, salt and beer. Knead until smooth. Let dough rise about 2 hours. Divide dough into 4 balls. Roll each ball ¼ inch thick and place in 4 ungreased 8 inch cake pans. Edges should be ¾ inch up the sides of the pans. Salt the dough in the pans and sprinkle with parmesan cheese.

Place one layer of mozzarella cheese on top and cover with about 4 tomatoes. Sprinkle with heavy shakes of oregano, basil, salt and pepper. Cover with meat mixture and press down with back of spoon. Top with heavy shakes of parmesan cheese. Bake at 450° for 30-35 minutes. Watch carefully. Cut and serve hot.

For freezing bake for 18-20 minutes and then freeze. When needed, reheat for about 30 minutes.

Four 8-inch pizzas

May also add sliced mushrooms, onions, ripe olives, green pepper, anchovies or whatever suits your pizza.

TOSTADO PIZZA

Show ■
Go □

2 T. yellow cornmeal
2 c. Bisquick
½ c. cold water
1 lb. ground beef
¾ c. water
3 T. chopped green chilies or green
   pepper
1 (6¼ oz.) pkg. taco seasoning mix
1 (15 ½ oz.) can refried beans
2½ c. shredded cheddar cheese
fresh chili peppers (optional)
1 c. shredded lettuce
1 c. chopped tomato
½ c. chopped onion
taco sauce

Generously grease a 12 inch pizza pan. Sprinkle with cornmeal. In large bowl combine Bisquick and ½ cup cold water. Stir with fork until dough follows fork around the bowl. Turn out on lightly floured surface. Knead 5 or 6 times. Roll to 14 inch circle and pat into prepared pizza pan. Crimp edges.

In skillet, brown meat; drain off fat. Add ¾ cup water, green chilies and taco seasoning mix; bring to a boil. Reduce heat and simmer uncovered for 15 minutes or until mixture is thick. Spread refried beans on dough. Spread meat mixture evenly over the beans.

Bake at 450° for 18-20 minutes. Sprinkle with cheddar cheese. Return to oven about 4 minutes or until cheese is melted. Cut and garnish with fresh peppers. Pass lettuce, tomato, onion and taco sauce.

6 slices

The best of two worlds

HOT MEXICAN LASAGNA

Show ■
Go ■

1½ lbs. ground beef
1 med. onion, chopped
1½ tsp ground cumin
2 cloves garlic, crushed
3 tsp. chili powder
1½ tsp. salt
½ tsp. pepper
¾ c. water
2 c. hot taco sauce
12 corn tortilla
1 lb. Monterey Jack cheese, shredded
1 (8 oz.) carton dairy sour cream

In large skillet, sauté beef and onion, stirring occasionally. Drain of drippings and add all seasonings and water. Simmer uncovered, stirring occasionally until most liquid has evaporated, about 10 minutes.

Pour ½ cup taco sauce into greased 9x13-inch baking dish. Arrange half of the tortillas to cover the bottom of the pan. Pour ½ cup taco sauce evenly over tortillas. Spoon on all of the beef mixture; top with sour cream applied in even "dollops" over the beef. Sprinkle with ½ of shredded cheese. Arrange remaining tortillas, overlapping slightly, on cheese. Spread remaining taco sauce over tortillas and top with rest of cheese. Cover with foil and bake at 375° for 40 minutes. Remove foil and bake 5 more minutes. Let casserole stand for 5 minutes before eating.

8-10 servings

Some like it "not hot" so use mild taco sauce.

SPICY BEEF AND PEANUTS

Show ■
Go ■

1 lb. flank steak, sliced into 2x¼-inch strips

Marinade:
1 T. dark soy sauce
1 T. cornstarch
1 T. oil

Sauce:
1 tsp. cornstarch
1 T. dry sherry
1½ T. dark soy sauce
2 tsp. red wine vinegar
2 tsp. sugar
1 tsp. sesame oil
2 c. oil
2-4 dried chili peppers, to taste
3 slices peeled gingerroot (size of a
    (quarter) finely chopped
½ c. unsalted peanuts
1 green onion, sliced

Place beef in bowl with marinade made of soy sauce, cornstarch and oil. Refrigerate 30 minutes. Combine sauce ingredients and set aside.

One hour before serving, heat 2 cups oil in wok over high heat. Add meat and fry quickly 2 minutes or until no longer pink. Drain and let cool. Reheat wok and add 2 tablespoons oil; reduce heat. Add chili peppers and press into oil until they darken. Add ginger and stir. Increase heat and stir fry meat with spicy oil. Mix sauce well and pour over meat until evenly coated. Add peanuts. To serve, garnish with sliced onion.

3-4 servings

Sliced chicken breasts instead of beef are a nice change.

This gets raves!

PSEUDO PRAKAS

Show ■
Go ☐

1 med. cabbage, shredded
3 lbs. ground beef
1 jumbo or 2 small eggs
1 c. bread crumbs
2 tsp. salt
⅛ tsp. garlic powder
freshly ground pepper
1 (10 oz.) bottle chili sauce
½-⅔ c. water
1 (16 oz.) can whole cranberries
1 (8 oz.) can tomato sauce (optional)

Place cabbage in large roasting pan. Combine meat, eggs, bread crumbs, salt, garlic powder and pepper; shape into small balls. Place on top of cabbage. Mix chili sauce, water, cranberries and tomato sauce together; pour over meatballs. Cover and bake at 350° for 3 hours. Excellent frozen and reheated.

8 servings

MEAT LOAF WELLINGTON

Show ■
Go ☐

4 lbs. ground beef
2 eggs
½ c. ketchup
½ envelope dry onion soup mix
salt and pepper
1 tsp. garlic powder
¼-½ c. Italian flavored bread crumbs
1 (2½ oz.) jar sliced mushrooms, drained
1 c. shredded cheddar cheese
2 pre-rolled Pepperidge Farm puff pastry
    sheets, thawed
1 egg, beaten
1 T. water

Mix together meat, eggs, ketchup, onion soup, salt, pepper, garlic powder, parmesan cheese and bread crumbs. Bake in 2 ungreased 5x9 inch loaf pans at 350 degrees for 30 minutes. Line a jelly roll pan with foil. Drain off juice from baked meat loaves; invert loaves on jelly roll pan. Top meat loaves with mushrooms and cheddar cheese; pat down well. Roll out pastry sheets and place on top of the loaves. Make sure sides are well covered. Brush tops with egg and water mixture. Bake at 400° for 30-35 minutes or until nicely browned. Loaves may be frozen.

10 servings

VARIATIONS ON A THEME

BEEF TENDERLOIN VARIATION I

Show ■
Go ■

1 (3½-4 lb.) whole beef tenderloin
2 T. butter or margarine
¼ c. chopped green onions
2 T. butter
2 T. soy sauce
1 tsp. Dijon mustard
freshly ground pepper
¾ c. sherry

Spread tenderloin with 2 tablespoons butter. Place on a rack in a shallow baking pan. Bake uncovered at 400° for 20 minutes. Meanwhile, in a small saucepan, cook green onions in 2 tablespoons butter until tender. Add soy sauce, mustard and pepper. Stir in sherry and heat just to boiling. Pour over tenderloin and bake 20-25 minutes for rare to medium beef. Baste several times with sauce. Extra sauce may be passed

10-12 servings

BEEF TENDERLOIN VARIATION II

Show ■
Go ■

1 (3 ½-4 lb.) whole beef tenderloin
Jane's Krazy Mixed-up Salt
ketchup
butter or margarine

Season beef to taste. Pour ketchup on top of roast, just until it begins to drip down the sides. Place large chunks of butter on top, every 2-3 inches. Amount of butter is dependent on size of meat. Be generous! Ketchup and butter will caramelize during baking. Bake at 425° for 25-35 minutes depending on the size of the meat. This dish is best served rare or medium rare.

10-12 servings

BEEF TENDERLOIN VARIATION III

Show ■
Go ■

1 (3 ½-4 lb.) whole beef tenderloin
salt and pepper
garlic powder
Lawry's seasoned salt
lemon pepper
soy sauce
Worcestershire sauce
1 (8 oz.) bottle Caesar salad dressing

Generously season tenderloin with salt, pepper, garlic powder, seasoned salt and lemon pepper. Sprinkle with soy sauce and Worcestershire. Pour dressing over meat and marinate in refrigerator overnight. Before cooking, drain off marinade. Bake at 450° for 20-30 minutes, depending on size of meat.

10-12 servings

SPANISH TONGUE

Show ■
Go ☐

1 (2½-3 lb.) fresh tongue
½ tsp. salt
½ tsp. pepper
3 whole cloves
½ tsp. cinnamon
½ tsp. nutmeg
3 celery tops
½ med. onion
3 ribs celery, sliced
3 carrots, peeled and sliced
1 med. onion, chopped
2 tsp. butter
1 (10½ oz.) pkg. frozen peas, thawed
1 (10½ oz.) can tomato soup
2 tsp. brown sugar

Place tongue in large pot and cover with water. Add salt, pepper, cloves, cinnamon, nutmeg, celery tops and ½ onion; simmer until tender, about 3 hours. Remove tongue; partially cool and remove skin. Save and strain liquid. Lightly sauté the celery, carrots and chopped onion in butter. Add peas. Cut tongue in thin slices and add to vegetables. Add tomato soup, 2-3 cups strained liquid and brown sugar; simmer uncovered 30 minutes or bake in casserole at 325° for 45 minutes. Serve with broad noodles or rice.

4-6 servings

Try adding canned mushrooms, sautéed green pepper or canned corn niblets.

SUMPTUOUS SHORT RIBS

Show ■
Go ☐

6 lbs. bone-in beef short ribs, cut into
    serving pieces
2 c. teriyaki sauce
2 c. prune juice
1 c. water
½ tsp. whole black peppercorns
3-4 medium onions, sliced
1 T. blackstrap molasses

Place the meat in a container and cover with a mixture of the teriyaki sauce and prune juice. Cover and refrigerate overnight or up to one day. Remove the ribs from the marinade and set aside. In a large pot, combine the marinade, water and peppercorns. Bring the mixture to a boil, reduce heat to medium low and cook for 30 minutes. In a roasting pan, layer the bottom with sliced onions. Add the meat and cover. Bake in a 350° oven for 2-3 hours or until the meat is very tender or falls away from the bone. Transfer the cooked meat and onions to a platter. Pour the sauce in a saucepan, add the molasses and cook for 5-10 minutes or until it is syrupy. Pour it over the meat and serve hot. Good with buttered noodles.

6 servings

OUTRAGEOUS BEEF TENDERLOIN

Show ■
Go ☐

3-4 lbs. beef tenderloin

Marinade:
4 oz. scotch
½ c. Worcestershire sauce
2 cloves fresh garlic, minced
fresh ground pepper

Coating:
¼ c. powdered sugar
¼ c. kosher salt

Combine marinade ingredients and add beef tenderloin. Marinate a minimum of 2 hours, up to 24 hours, turning frequently. Remove beef from marinade. Combine powdered sugar and salt and spread on wax paper. Roll beef in mixture until well coated on all sides. For medium rare; grill beef on high for 7 minutes, turning four times, for a total of 28 minutes.

8-10 servings

CHICKEN BREAST WITH MUSTARD PERSILLADE

Show ■
Go ■

4 whole boned chicken breasts, cut in half
½ c. Dijon mustard

Persillade Coating:
½ c. butter
4 cloves garlic, crushed
2 c. bread crumbs (2 slices fresh bread)
⅔ c. minced parsley, firmly packed
salt and pepper

Rinse chicken under cold water and pat dry with paper towels. Place on large sheet of waxed paper. Brush skin side of each breast generously with mustard. To make persillade coating, sauté garlic in butter. Add crumbs and stir over medium heat until lightly browned. Mix in parsley and season to taste.

Carefully dip mustard sides into persillade and press firmly to make crumbs adhere. Place chicken breasts, crumb side up, in a baking dish. Bake at 425° for 25-30 minutes or until persillade coating is golden brown.

4-6 servings

Keep left over persillade refrigerated in airtight container for up to five days. May be frozen.

*What's persillade?
Try it, you'll like it!*

CHICKEN CHINESE

Show ■
Go ■

4 whole boned chicken breasts
1 (8 oz.) bottle Italian dressing
Jane's Krazy Mixed-up Salt
garlic powder
paprika
2 c. fried rice
1 (9½ oz.) jar sweet and sour sauce

Marinate chicken breasts in dressing overnight. Next day drain and season chicken with salt, garlic powder and paprika to taste. Place 1 heaping teaspoon of fried rice in center of each breast. Roll up and secure with toothpick. Place in 9x13-inch baking dish. Bake at 350° for 20 minutes. If skin is not crisp, place under broiler until golden brown and crisp. Pour sweet and sour sauce to cover chicken breasts. Bake 20 minutes more or until tender. Large chicken breasts may take longer.

4-6 servings

Remaining rice may be served on the side.

THE PLANNERS CHICKEN DIJONNAISE

Show ■
Go ■

4 (6 oz.) chicken breasts, boned, skinned
    and pounded
Dijon mustard
flour
3 T. butter
¼ c. dry white wine
1 c. whipping cream
1 T. Dijon mustard
salt and pepper

Spread chicken breasts lightly on both sides with mustard. Dredge in flour and shake off excess. Brown in butter over medium heat on both sides about 4-5 minutes per side. Remove to a heatproof platter and keep warm. Pour wine into skillet and boil rapidly, scraping up brown bits. Add cream and boil 2-3 minutes or until slightly thickened. Stir in 1 tablespoon mustard, salt and pepper to taste. Pour over chicken and serve.

4 servings

CHICKEN MADEIRA

Show ■
Go ☐

4 whole boned chicken breasts, skinned and cut in half
salt and pepper
garlic powder
½ c. flour
¼ c. butter

Madeira sauce:
½ c. butter
1 T. chopped onion
1 T. chopped celery
1 clove garlic, crushed
⅓ c. flour
2 (10½ oz.) cans beef broth plus ¼ c. water
2 oz. Madeira wine
1 oz. brandy
4-6 c. cooked wild rice
fresh parsley

Season chicken with salt, pepper and garlic powder to taste. Dredge in flour, shaking off excess. Sauté in ¼ cup butter until golden brown; set aside.

For Madeira sauce, melt ½ cup butter in large skillet to foaming consistency. Add onion, celery, garlic and sauté for about 5 minutes. Blend in flour and add beef broth, wine and brandy. Cover, bring to a boil and simmer about 30 minutes. Strain and check seasonings.

Cut chicken pieces in half and place in hot Madeira sauce until chicken is heated through and coated with sauce. Place chicken pieces over rice and garnish with fresh parsley.

4-6 servings

Lobster can be used along with chicken.

COMPANY CHICKEN

Show ■
Go ■

6 whole chicken breasts
¼ c. butter, melted
salt and pepper to taste
garlic powder
2 (10¾ oz.) cans cream of chicken soup
¾ c. Sautérne wine
¼ c. water
4 oz. fresh mushrooms, sliced
1 (8 oz.) can sliced water chestnuts
¾ c. green grapes
1 c. chopped parsley

Brush chicken with butter and season well with salt, pepper and garlic powder. Broil until brown, about 10 minutes per side; place in 9x13-inch baking pan. Combine soup, wine and water and pour over chicken. Cover with remaining ingredients. Bake covered at 350° for 1 hour. Uncover to brown last 15 minutes.

6 servings

CHICKEN MARAKESH

Show ■
Go ☐

8 lbs. cut-up chicken
seasoned salt
2 c. cornflake crumbs
½ c. butter
3 onions, sliced
1 (2 ¼ oz.) can sliced ripe olives
1 lb. fresh mushrooms, sliced
½ c. golden raisins
1 (16 oz.) can tomatoes
1½ c. white wine
2 c. white rice, cooked

Season chicken with salt and roll in corn- flake crumbs. In skillet, sauté chicken in butter until browned. Remove and place in roaster. Add onions to skillet and brown. Turn off heat and add olives, mushrooms, raisins, tomatoes and 1 cup wine. Pour mixture over chicken. Bake uncovered at 350° for 1 hour. Add ½ cup wine and bake 30 minutes longer. Baste while cooking. Serve over rice.

8 servings

CHICKEN PARMESAN

Show ■
Go ■

2 c. seasoned bread crumbs
¾ c. grated parmesan cheese
1 tsp. paprika
¼ c. finely chopped parsley
1 tsp. oregano
¼ tsp. basil
1-2 tsp. salt
⅛ tsp. pepper
2 (2½ -3 lb.) cut-up chickens
¾ c. butter or margarine, melted

Mix together bread crumbs, cheese, paprika, parsley, oregano, basil, salt and pepper. Dip chicken pieces into melted butter, then roll in bread crumb mixture until well coated. Arrange skin side up in a foil-lined shallow baking pan. Bake at 375° for 1-1½ hours until tender. Do not turn chicken pieces while baking.

8 servings

Additional parmesan cheese may be sprinkled on top before baking. Any Italian marinara sauce may be poured on top before baking.

CHICKEN AND PASTA

Show ■
Go ■

4 (8 oz.) chicken breasts, skinned and
    boned
¼-½ c. flour
3 eggs, beaten
⅓ c. oil
½ c. sliced fresh mushrooms
½ c. butter
1 tsp. salt
½ tsp. white pepper
garlic powder to taste
½ lb. fresh or dried fettucine noodles
    cooked al dente
½ c. whipping cream
½ c. milk
1 c. grated parmesan cheese
2 T. minced parsley

Dip chicken in flour, in eggs and then back in flour. Sauté in oil until golden brown. Dice chicken and set aside. In large skillet, sauté mushrooms in butter. Season with salt, pepper and garlic powder. Add the diced chicken. Mix in noodles, cream, milk and cheese. Serve on warmed plate and sprinkle with additional parmesan cheese and parsley.

4 servings

MARINATED CHICKEN

Show ■
Go ■

1 (2½ -3 lb.) cut-up chicken
1 clove garlic, crushed
⅔ c. water
¼ c. oil
2 T. lemon juice
2 T. spicy brown mustard
2 tsp. salt
½ tsp. chili powder
½ tsp. sugar (optional)

Place chicken in large bowl. Combine remaining ingredients and pour over chicken. Refrigerate for several hours or overnight, turning chicken two or three times. Drain and reserve marinade.

Preheat broiler for 10 minutes. Put chicken, skin side down, on broiler pan or charcoal grill. Brush with marinade and broil 20 minutes on each side, basting with marinade every 5 minutes.

4-5 servings

Chicken with a kick!

CHICKEN IN FILLO WITH MADEIRA SAUCE

Show ■
Go ■

3 whole boned chicken breasts, skinned
    and cut in half
salt and pepper

Mushroom Filling:
1 lb. fresh mushrooms, finely chopped
3 T. onion, chopped
¼ c. unsalted butter
salt
pepper
4-5 tsp. Madeira wine
¼ c. whipping cream
1 pkg. fillo leaves
1 c. unsalted butter, melted

Madeira Sauce:
3 T. butter
1½ T. flour
¾ c. beef stock
1 tsp. Kitchen Bouquet
¼ c. Madeira wine
¼ c. reserved Mushroom Filling

Make a slit, lengthwise in each chicken breast. Place in well-greased baking dish. Season with salt and pepper. Put parchment paper over chicken and tuck into sides of dish. Bake at 450° for 7 minutes. Remove from baking dish and cool.

For filling, over high heat, sauté mushrooms, onion, butter, salt and pepper. Pour in wine and cream. Cook about 5 minutes until mixture coats mushrooms; let cool. Fill each chicken breast with mushroom mixture, reserving ¼ cup for sauce.

Remove 2 sheets of fillo and cover the rest with a damp towel. Brush each sheet with melted butter. Place one chicken breast on the 2 sheets and wrap with dough starting at the narrow edge. Continue to brush dough with butter as you fold. Place seam side down on well greased cookie sheet. Repeat with remaining chicken breasts. Bake at 350° for 20 minutes or until brown. Do not overcook.

For Madeira sauce, melt butter; stir in flour, beef stock and Kitchen Bouquet. Cook 5 minutes. Add Madeira and cook until thickened. Stir in ¼ cup mushroom mixture. Before serving, pour 2 tablespoons hot Madeira sauce over each chicken breast.

6 servings

May be prepared day ahead except for baking

MEXICAN CHICKEN

Show ■
Go ■

4 whole boned chicken breasts, skinned
    and cut in half
8 small chunks Monterey Jack cheese
1 egg, beaten
1 c. bread crumbs
2 T. butter or margarine
1 onion, chopped
1 (6 oz.) can pitted ripe olives
1 (14 oz.) can mild enchilada sauce
2 c. shredded cheddar cheese
crumbled taco chips

Pound chicken breasts thin. Place a chunk of cheese on each breast and shape chicken around it. Dip into egg and then bread crumbs. Melt butter and sauté chicken until lightly browned. Place in 9x13-inch pan, seam side down, and cover with onion, olives and enchilada sauce. Top with cheese and taco chips. Bake at 350° for 1 hour or until bubbly.

6 servings

Chicken can be prepared ahead and baked just before serving.

PURPLE PLUM CHICKEN

Show ■
Go ■

2 (3 lb.) cut-up chickens
garlic and onion salt

Sauce:
1 onion, chopped
3 T. oil
1 (30 oz.) can purple plums, drained and
    pureed
1 (6 oz.) can frozen lemonade concentrate
⅓ c. chili sauce
¼ c. soy sauce
1 tsp. ginger
2 drops Tabasco
1 tsp. Worcestershire
1½ tsp. dry mustard

Place seasoned chicken, skin side up, on foil-lined greased baking pan or broiler pan with sides and broil until browned. For sauce, sauté onion in oil. Combine remaining ingredients, add to onion and simmer 10 minutes. Pour ½ of sauce over browned chicken. Bake at 350° for 45 minutes, basting frequently with remaining sauce.

6-8 servings

Sauce can also be used for duck and Cornish hens.

TOULOUSE CHICKEN

Show ■
Go ☐

Marinade:
2 c. oil
½ c. dry white wine
½ tsp. salt
¼ tsp. oregano
¼ tsp. garlic powder
4 whole boned chicken breasts, cut in half

Seasoned butter:
1 c. butter, softened
1 clove garlic, chopped
½ tsp. chopped green onion
¼ tsp. Dijon mustard
dash each or curry powder, thyme,
    cumin,nutmeg
¾ tsp. chopped almonds
1 T. chopped parsley
½ T. Pernod liqueur
salt and pepper to taste

2 T. oil
¼ tsp. oregano
¼ c. chopped ripe olives
¼ c. pimento-stuffed olives
⅓ c. chopped canned tomatoes

Combine all ingredients for marinade. Place chicken breasts in mixture; cover and refrigerate overnight.

Next day, make seasoned butter by combining listed ingredients. Remove chicken from marinade and brown in 2 tablespoons oil over high heat, skin side up, for 4-5 minutes. Turn and season with ¼ teaspoon oregano. Reduce heat, cover and cook 5-8 minutes longer or until done. Melt seasoned butter mixture in a saucepan, adding olives and tomatoes. Cook on high heat stirring constantly. Place chicken on serving plate and cover with ½ of the sauce. Pass remaining sauce.

8 servings

The chicken you'd cross the road for...

CHICKEN CACCIATORE

Show ■
Go ■

6 whole chicken breasts
salt
pepper
2 T. olive oil
2 cloves garlic, crushed
8 oz. fresh mushrooms, sliced
1 med. onion, chopped
1 med. green pepper, chopped
1 (28 oz.) can stewed tomatoes
1 (6 oz.) can tomato paste (optional)
1 (2¼ oz.) can sliced ripe olives
1 (2¼ oz.) can sliced green olives
celery seed

Season chicken with salt and pepper. Brown in olive oil with crushed garlic. Add mushrooms, onion, green pepper and sauté until limp. Place mixture in roasting pan and add remaining ingredients. Cook uncovered until sauce reaches spaghetti sauce consistency, approximately 45-55 minutes. Serve over parsley buttered new potatoes, buttered noodles or wild rice.

6 servings

HONEY CURRY CHICKEN

Show ■
Go ■

½ c. butter
½ c. honey
¼ c. prepared mustard
2 tsp. curry powder
pinch of salt
4 whole chicken breasts

In saucepan, melt butter and add honey, mustard, curry powder and salt. Place chicken breasts, skin side up, in 9x13-inch pan. Bake at 350° for 15 minutes. Baste with sauce and continue baking for 1 hour, basting with sauce every 15 minutes until done.

4 servings

BROWN SUGAR CURED TURKEY

Show ■
Go ☐

1 - 20 lb. turkey
½ c. packed golden brown sugar
¼ c. kosher salt
2 tsp. onion powder
1 tsp. garlic powder
1 tsp. poultry seasoning
2 large onions, quartered
4 c. chicken broth

Rinse turkey inside and out. Pat dry with paper towels. Place turkey on a platter. Mix brown sugar, salt, powders and poultry seasoning and blend well. Rub salt mixture all over outside of turkey. Refrigerate turkey uncovered for 24 hours. Position rack in bottom third of oven and preheat to 300°. Arrange onion quarters in large roasting pan. Place turkey on top of onions. Tie legs together and tuck wings under turkey. Sprinkle with pepper. Cover loosely with foil. Roast turkey for 2 hours. Uncover and roast for 30 minutes. Add 2 cups of chicken broth to roasting pan and baste turkey with broth. Roast 1 hour, basting every 20 minutes. Add another 2 cups of broth to roasting pan and continue to baste frequently (every 20 minutes) for about an hour and roast until dark brown. Cover turkey loosely with foil: continue to roast until thermometer inserted to innermost part of thigh registers 180°, about 1½ hours longer. Transfer turkey to a platter. Tent with foil and let stand 30 minutes before carving.

10 servings

SIMPLY INCREDIBLE CHICKEN

Show ■
Go ■

1 chicken, quartered
garlic salt
½-1 c. brown sugar

Arrange chicken skin side up on a lightly oiled baking pan. Season chicken generously with garlic salt and brown sugar. Bake in preheated 375° oven for 1 hour. Cover with foil after 30-45 minutes if chicken appears too dry.

2-3 servings

SZECHUAN CHICKEN STIR FRY

Show ■
Go ■

1 lb. skinless, boneless chicken breasts, cut into 1 inch pieces
6 T. cornstarch
2 cloves garlic, chopped
6 T. vegetable oil
1 bunch green onions, chopped

Sauce:
5 T. soy sauce
3 T. white wine vinegar
1½ tsp. white sugar
⅓ tsp. cayenne pepper

Put cornstarch in a gallon sized plastic bag. Add chicken and coat completely. Put oil in the frying pan along with the garlic and heat to a sizzle. Add chicken pieces and fry for approx. 5 minutes until golden. Remove chicken from pan and wipe out the frying pan. Combine sauce ingredients. Put the chicken back in the pan and add the sauce to glaze the chicken for about 60 seconds. Remove from heat. Serve with chopped green onions.

4 servings

BUTTERMILK OVEN-FRIED CHICKEN

Show ■
Go ■

1½ c. buttermilk
⅓ c. extra virgin olive oil
3 T. hot pepper sauce
2 T. Dijon mustard
2 cloves garlic, minced
1 tsp. kosher salt
½ tsp. black pepper
1 lg. onion, sliced
12 chicken pieces with skin and bones
5 T. melted butter
1 c. dry unseasoned bread crumbs
1/3 c. freshly grated parmesan cheese
¼ c. flour
½ tsp. paprika
½ tsp. cayenne pepper
1 tsp. salt

Whisk buttermilk, oil, hot pepper sauce, mustard, garlic, salt and pepper in a large bowl to blend well. Add sliced onion, then chicken pieces and turn to coat. Cover, chill at least 3 hours or overnight. Turn chicken occasionally. Blend bread crumbs, cheese, flour, paprika, cayenne and salt in a baking dish. Remove chicken from marinade, allowing excess to drip off. Place chicken in crumb mixture and turn to coat completely. Place wire racks on 2 large rimmed baking sheets. Arrange chicken, skin side up on racks. Let stand for 30 minutes. Drizzle butter over chicken. Bake 45 minutes at 400° until crisp, golden and cooked through.

6 servings

TROUT AMANDINE

Show ■
Go ■

2½ lbs. trout fillets, skinned
½ c. milk
½ c. flour
salt and pepper, to taste
1 c. butter
6 oz. almonds, roasted
juice of 2 lemons
1 T. chopped parsley

Dip fillets into milk, then dredge in flour, salt and pepper. Melt butter in skillet and fry fillets slowly until brown on both sides. Remove to a warm platter. Sprinkle almonds over fish. Add juice and parsley to skillet and cook a few minutes. Pour sauce over fish and serve.

6 servings

BAKED ITALIAN TROUT

Show ■
Go ■

1 (5 lb.) trout, skinned and boned
salt and pepper, to taste
1 egg, slightly beaten
1 c. bread crumbs
grated parmesan cheese, to taste

Season fish with salt and pepper. Dip in egg, then bread crumbs. Sprinkle with parmesan cheese. Bake at 400° for 10-20 minutes.

5-6 servings

BAKED TROUT IN WINE

Show ■
Go ■

6 rainbow trout, dressed and washed
2 T. lemon juice
salt and pepper, to taste
1 c. dry white wine
2 T. chopped parsley
¼ c. sliced green onion
2 T. dry bread crumbs
¼ c. melted butter
fresh dill
6 thin lemon slices

Brush inside of trout with lemon juice and sprinkle with salt and pepper. Arrange trout in shallow baking dish and brush with remaining lemon juice; sprinkle with salt and pepper. Pour wine into baking dish. Cover fish with parsley and onion. Sprinkle with bread crumbs and spoon butter over each fish. Bake uncovered at 400° for 25 minutes or until flaky. Arrange on platter and garnish with dill and lemon slices.

6 servings

ELEGANT CRAB ASPARAGUS

Show ■
Go ☐

⅓ c. butter
⅓ c. flour
1¼ c. milk
1 tsp. seasoned salt
¼ tsp. pepper
¼ c. grated parmesan cheese
2 (6 oz.) pkgs. frozen king crab, thawed
   and drained
2 (15 oz.) cans colossal white asparagus
   spears
grated parmesan cheese
paprika

For sauce, melt butter over low heat and stir in flour until well blended. Add milk and stir constantly. Add salt, pepper and parmesan cheese and continue cooking until smooth. Set aside. Place crab in greased 2 quart casserole. Sprinkle with salt and pepper if desired. Add ½ cup sauce and mix with crabmeat. Arrange asparagus spears on top and spoon remaining sauce over all. Sprinkle with parmesan cheese and paprika. Bake at 375° for 30 minutes or until bubbly.

4 servings

Serve with fruit or salad.

SAUCY SHRIMP

Show ■
Go ☐

1½ lbs. fresh mushrooms, cleaned
2 T. butter
1 (20 oz.) can artichoke hearts
1 lb. med. shrimp, cooked

Sauce:
6½ T. butter
4½ T. flour
1½ c. half and half cream
salt and pepper, to taste
½ c. sherry
1 T. Worcestershire sauce
½ c. grated parmesan cheese
paprika

Sauté mushrooms in 2 tablespoons butter. Arrange half the artichokes on bottom of 1½-2 quart casserole. Place shrimp and mushrooms over artichokes. Prepare sauce by melting butter in pan and adding flour and cream and stirring constantly. When thickened, season with salt and pepper and add sherry and Worcestershire. Pour sauce in casserole. Arrange remaining artichokes on top of sauce and sprinkle with parmesan cheese and paprika. Bake at 375° for 20 minutes.

4-6 servings

BUTTERFLIED WOKERY SHRIMP

Show ■
Go ■

2 lbs. raw shrimp, cleaned and deveined
2 egg whites
2 T. sherry
2 T. cornstarch
½ c. oil
4 tsp. finely chopped fresh ginger
4 tsp. crushed garlic
¼ tsp. chili pepper
4 green onions, chopped
1 tsp. salt
2 T. soy sauce
½ c. ketchup
4 tsp. sugar
4 tsp. cornstarch
½ c. water
2 c. cooked long grain rice

Slit each shrimp part way down the back. Combine egg whites, sherry and 2 tablespoons cornstarch. Marinate shrimp in mixture for 30 minutes. Heat oil in wok and stir-fry ginger, garlic, chili pepper and onions 2-3 minutes. Add marinated shrimp and stir-fry 2-4 minutes longer. Add salt, soy sauce, ketchup and sugar and cook a few minutes, being careful not to overcook. Mix 4 teaspoons cornstarch and water; add to shrimp and cook until thickened. Serve with or over white rice.

4-6 servings

For hotter tastes use more chili pepper.

They'd wok a mile for this dish

COLD FILLET OF FISH ROMANOFF

Show ■
Go ☐

6 fillets of sole or flounder, cut in half (about 3 lbs.)

Court Bouillon:
1 qt. water
1 c. white wine
½ rib celery
1 bay leaf
1 small onion, quartered
½ lemon
6 peppercorns
1 clove garlic, crushed
1 tsp. salt

Sauce:
¾ c. dairy sour cream
¾ c. mayonnaise
¼ tsp. Dijon mustard
1½ tsp. lemon juice
¼ tsp. salt
¼ tsp. pepper
1 clove garlic, crushed
1 shallot, minced
1 (2oz.) jar red caviar
6 lemon wedges

Roll each fillet and secure with toothpick. Bring court bouillon to a boil in a 10 inch skillet. Reduce heat and simmer for 5 minutes uncovered. Place fish rolls in skillet. Cover and cook 5-6 minutes or until tender. Drain and refrigerate overnight.

Combine sauce ingredients in a small bowl, refrigerate for 6 hours or overnight.

The next day place fish rolls on serving plate. Spoon some of the sauce over fish. Sprinkle each roll with caviar, garnish with lemon wedges. Serve with remaining sauce.

4-6 servings

This must be made the day before serving.

A two day operation

CIOPPINO – SAN FRANCISCO FISH STEW

Show ■
Go ☐

8 green onions, sliced
2 cloves garlic, chopped
1 c. chopped celery
20 fresh mushrooms
⅓ c. olive oil
⅓ c. chopped parsley
1 c. canned tomato puree
1 (8 oz.) can tomato sauce
1 (6 oz.) can tomato paste
2½ c. water
2 c. Sautérne wine
1 tsp. lemon juice
1 bay leaf
1½ tsp. salt
¼ tsp. pepper
½ tsp. allspice
2 lbs. clams, in shell, well scrubbed
¾ lb. raw shrimp, cleaned and deveined
1 lb. red snapper or halibut fillet, cut
    into 1-inch chunks
¾-1 lb. crabmeat

In a 6-8 quart pot, sauté onions, garlic, celery and mushrooms in oil. Add all remaining ingredients except fish and seafood. Bring to a boil; reduce heat and simmer for 2 hours. Add clams and cook until shells open. Add shrimp and snapper and cook until fish flakes easily. Add crabmeat and heat thoroughly.

Types and amounts of seafood may vary. Great served with thick slices of garlic bread.

6 servings

JAMBALAYA

Show ■
Go ■

1 lb. smoked salami or beer sticks, cubed
½ c. oil
2 med. onions, chopped
8 green onions, chopped
1 lb. fresh mushrooms, sliced
1 lg. green pepper, chopped
½ c. diced celery
¼ tsp. thyme
2 bay leaves
4 cloves garlic
½ tsp. salt
dash red cayenne pepper
2 lbs. raw shrimp, peeled and deveined
2 (16 oz.) cans tomatoes, including
     liquid
1 (6 oz.) can tomato paste
½ lemon, quartered
3 cups cooked long grain rice

In a 4-quart Dutch oven, brown salami in hot oil. Add onions, mushrooms, green pepper, celery, thyme, bay leaves, garlic, salt and red pepper. Cook 3 minutes. Add shrimp, tomatoes, tomato paste and lemon. Simmer slowly, uncovered, tossing ingredients often until shrimp is pink. Remove bay leaves and lemon. Add rice and toss all together; serve.

8-10 servings

A New Orleans specialty

SALMON MOUSSE

Show ■
Go ☐

1 (8 oz.) pkg. cream cheese
1 (10 ¾ oz.) can tomato soup
2½ T. unflavored gelatin
½ c. cold water
1 c. mayonnaise
1 (16 oz.) can red salmon, drained and
   flaked
½ c. finely chopped celery
½ c. finely chopped green pepper

Sauce:
1 c. dairy sour cream
1-2 T. dry onion soup mix
½ c. diced cucumber

Heat cream cheese and soup until creamy. Beat with rotary beater. Dissolve gelatin in water and mix into soup. When cool, add mayonnaise. Fold in salmon, celery, green pepper and pour into oiled 2½-quart dish or fish mold. Refrigerate overnight.

For sauce, combine sour cream, onion soup mix and cucumber. Serve in separate bowl.

16 servings

Great luncheon dish or appetizer with toast rounds. May substitute 3 (7 oz.) cans of water packed tuna for salmon.

SALMON PATTIES

Show ☐
Go ■

1 (16 oz.) can red salmon, drained and
   flaked
4 eggs, slightly beaten
salt and pepper to taste
1 c. dairy sour cream
1 c. crushed corn flakes
2 T. minced green onions
oil for frying

Mix all ingredients except oil in bowl. Place in refrigerator for 15 minutes. Shape mixture into patties. Fry until brown on one side. Turn and brown other side.

12 patties

May top with fried mushrooms and onions or Mushroom Sauce (see index). Also good cold.

ROASTED SALMON FILET WITH CUCUMBER SOUR CREAM SAUCE

Show ■
Go ■

⅓ c. dry white wine
⅓ c. orange juice
⅓ c. soy sauce
36 oz. salmon filet (whole or cut into six pieces) skin removed
sea salt, to taste

Cucumber Sour Cream Sauce:
1 c. packed baby spinach leaves
1 c. packed baby arugula leaves
½ shallot
¾ c. sour cream
3 T. Dijon mustard
½ c. chopped, seeded, and peeled cucumber

Mix wine, orange juice and soy sauce. Place salmon in 9x13 inch glass baking dish. Pour marinade over to cover fish. Place plastic wrap over dish and refrigerate for 3 hours. Turn occasionally. Preheat oven to 450°. Line baking sheet with foil. Shake off excess marinade and place salmon on baking sheet. Roast until fish is opaque in center approximately 15 minutes. Sprinkle with sea salt.

Finely chop spinach, arugula, and shallot in processor. Add sour cream and mustard; process until just blended. Transfer to medium bowl. Cover and refrigerate. Stir cucumber into sour cream mixture. Season to taste with salt and pepper.

6 servings

MAPLE GLAZED SALMON

Show ■
Go ■

¼ c. maple syrup
¼ c. low sodium soy sauce
¼ c. rice vinegar
2 T. olive oil
2 cloves fresh garlic, crushed
4 skinless salmon steaks
salt and pepper, to taste

Combine first 5 ingredients. Cook over high heat until mixture reduces by ½. Season salmon with salt and pepper. Marinate for a minimum of three hours. Grill for best results or bake 400° for 15-20 minutes, until opaque in color.

4 servings

"GREEK STYLE" HALIBUT

Show ■
Go ☐

4 Italian plum tomatoes, seeded and diced
2 T. kalamata olives, chopped
⅓ c. drained capers
1 tsp. fresh minced garlic
3 T. virgin olive oil, divided
3 T. fresh lemon juice, divided
¼ c. dry white wine
½ c. crumbled Feta cheese, divided
2 T. minced shallots
2 T. chopped fresh basil
4 (6-8 oz.) halibut fillets
salt and pepper, to taste

In a bowl, combine tomatoes, olives, capers, garlic, 2 tablespoons of the olive oil, 2 tablespoons of the lemon juice, wine, ¼ cup of the feta, shallots, basil and salt and pepper. Let stand at room temperature for a minimum of 30 minutes until flavors blend.

Preheat oven to 425°. Line shallow baking tray (jelly roll pan) with foil and brush with olive oil. Season halibut fillets on both sides with salt and pepper and place on prepared pan. Drizzle remaining lemon juice over fillets and top with tomato mixture and ¼ cup of feta. Bake 15 minutes or until cooked through. Pour pan juices over fish before serving.

4 servings

BLACKENED HALIBUT

Show ■
Go ☐

1 lb. halibut steak, with skin removed
4 T. butter
½ c. chopped shallots
1 c. white wine
1 T. maple syrup

Blackening spices:
¼ tsp chili powder
½ tsp. dry mustard
½ tsp. thyme
½ tsp. garlic powder
1 T. sugar
½ tsp. salt
¼ tsp. pepper

Mix together blackening spices and set aside. Preheat oven to 350°. Using a large pan, over medium heat, sauté shallots in 1 T. butter until transparent. Add white wine, bring to a simmer and cook until reduced by about ½. Stir in blackening spices and maple syrup. Heat a cast iron skillet just large enough to hold the halibut steaks until very hot. Melt 1 T. butter per steak in pan. First pour in ½ of the white wine mixture. Add fish. Sear the fish for about 1 minute, allowing the liquid to almost completely evaporate. As the liquid disappears, the sugar caramelizes to give the fish the blackened finish and to seal in moisture. Add remaining tablespoon of butter and balance of white wine mixture. Flip the fish and sear for only one minute. Place skillet into preheated oven and bake for 10-15 minutes until fish is barely done. Serve immediately.

4 servings

ROSEMARY VEAL CHOPS

Show ■
Go ■

4 (½-in. thick) veal chops, boned
2 eggs, slightly beaten
1-2 tsp. rosemary
salt and pepper, to taste
1 c. bread crumbs
3 T. olive oil
2 T. butter
4 cloves garlic, halved

Pound veal between two pieces of waxed paper. Dip veal into beaten eggs. Sprinkle with rosemary, salt and pepper and dip into bread crumbs. In large skillet, heat oil, butter and garlic. Add veal and cook on medium to high heat about 15 minutes or until golden brown. Discard garlic and place chops on a serving dish.

4 servings

MINNESOTA VEAL STEW

Show ■
Go ■

4 lbs. veal shoulder or breast, boned
    and cubed
salt and pepper
¼ c. oil
2 c. finely chopped onions
1 T. chopped garlic
1 tsp. saffron (optional)
¼ c. flour
¼ c. dry white wine
1 (28 oz.) can peeled tomatoes, chopped
1 c. chicken broth
2 tsp. rosemary
buttered noodles or rice

Sprinkle veal with salt and pepper. Heat oil in a large Dutch oven. Add veal, cook for 20 minutes, stirring frequently until liquid evaporates and meat is browned. Add onions, garlic and saffron. Cook, stirring occasionally, about 5 minutes. Sprinkle with flour, stir to coat meat evenly. Add wine, tomatoes, broth, rosemary and salt and pepper to taste. Cover and bake at 375° for 1 hour. Serve over noodles or rice.

8 servings

a real Minnesota rouser

VEAL DAUBE

Show ☐
Go ■

1 (4-5 lb.) veal shoulder roast
1 clove garlic
¼ c. flour
1 tsp. salt
⅛ tsp. pepper
¼ tsp. allspice
½ tsp. each thyme and sage
2 bay leaves, crushed
oil for browning
1 med. onion, minced
4 carrots, sliced
2 ribs celery, including leaves, diced
1 c. boiling water

Rub roast all over with cut garlic and dredge roast in mixture of flour and spices. In a heavy pan, brown in oil until crust forms. Remove meat. Brown vegetable in same pan and return meat. Add boiling water, cover and cook slowly over low heat 2-2½ hours or until tender.

8 servings

BLUE HORSE VEAL PICCATA

Show ■
Go ■

12 (3 oz.) pieces veal sliced for scaloppine
salt
freshly ground pepper
1 c. flour
½ c. olive oil
¼ c. Shallot Butter (see index)
⅓ c.dry white wine
juice of 1 lemon
8 lemon slices
2 T. chopped parsley

Pound veal slices until thin. Sprinkle with salt and pepper and dredge lightly in flour. Heat olive oil in a large skillet and sauté veal on both sides until lightly browned. Transfer to a hot platter. Pour off oil from pan and add Shallot Butter, wine and lemon juice. When butter has melted and the liquid begins to boil, return veal to pan. Turn pieces frequently, allowing the sauce to reduce to a glazed consistency. Remove veal, place on hot platter and top with reduced sauce. Garnish with lemon slices and fresh chopped parsley.

6 servings

VEAL SUPREME

Show ■
Go ☐

1½ lbs. veal cutlets, pounded slightly
½ c. flour
garlic powder, to taste
pinch of salt
2 eggs, beaten
2 T. milk
¾ c. bread crumbs
¼ c. oil
2 (8 oz.) jars marinara sauce

Cheese Topping:
3 T. butter
3 T. flour
½ tsp. salt
1½ c. milk
4 oz. Gruyere cheese, cut in chunks
¼ c. grated parmesan cheese
parmesan cheese and paprika for garnish

Dredge veal in mixture of flour, garlic powder and salt. Combine eggs and 2 tablespoons milk and dip veal first in eggs and then in bread crumbs. Brown in oil on both sides. Pour marinara sauce into a large pan and place veal in sauce.

For topping, melt butter in saucepan, add flour, salt, 1½ cups milk, Gruyere and parmesan cheeses. Stir well to blend and pour sauce over veal. Garnish with more parmesan cheese and paprika. Bake uncovered at 350° for 45 minutes or until brown.

6 servings

LEMON VEAL

Show ■
Go ■

2 lbs. veal sliced for scaloppine
2 eggs, beaten
½ c. flour
½ c. butter
1 lemon

Dip veal in eggs and then in flour. Sauté in butter in large skillet, turning until brown on both sides. Remove and place on serving platter. Squeeze lemon juice into hot pan, stir and pour over veal.

4 servings

Serve with buttered noodles and fried zucchini.

VEAL MARSALA

Show ■
Go ■

2 lbs. veal sliced for scaloppine
1 c. flour
¼ c. butter
garlic salt
salt
pepper
2 (10 oz.) cans beef consomme
¼ c. Marsala wine
1 lg. onion, chopped
1 med. green pepper, chopped
½ lb. fresh mushrooms, sliced
2 (8 oz.) pkgs. noodles, cooked al dente

Dredge veal in flour. Melt butter in a large skillet and brown veal lightly on both sides. Season with salts and pepper. Add consomme and simmer uncovered 10-15 minutes. Add wine and simmer uncovered 2-3 minutes. Place veal in a 9x13-inch baking dish or casserole and cover with pan juices. Sauté onion, pepper and mushrooms and spread over veal. Bake at 325°, uncovered, for 20 minutes. Serve over noodles.

6-8 servings

VEAL, PEPPERS AND ONIONS

Show ■
Go ■

2½ lbs. veal sliced for scaloppine
3 eggs, beaten
1 c. bread crumbs
½ c. olive oil
1 c. sherry
1 c. water
6 beef bouillon cubes
½ lb. fresh mushrooms, sliced
3 cloves garlic, peeled
2 (7 oz.) jars Progresso sweet peppers
    and onions

Dip veal in eggs and then into bread crumbs. Sauté in oil until browned on both sides. In a saucepan, bring sherry, water and bouillon cubes to a boil. Add mushrooms, garlic, peppers and onions. Place veal in a 9x13-inch baking dish. Pour sherry mixture over the veal; remove garlic cloves. Bake at 350° for 30 minutes.

8 servings

VEAL PARMIGIANI

Show ■
Go □

Sauce:
5 T. oil
1 lg. onion, chopped
2 cloves garlic, mashed
2 (16 oz.) cans tomato sauce
½ c. water
1 tsp. basil
1 tsp. oregano
½ tsp. seasoned salt
¼ tsp. sugar
¼ tsp. pepper
2 T. chopped parsley
1 lb. veal, sliced for scaloppine
½ c. grated parmesan cheese
½ c. fine dry bread crumbs
2 eggs, slightly beaten
¼ c. oil
1 (16 oz.) pkg. mozzarella cheese, sliced
3 T. grated parmesan cheese
2 (8 oz.) pkgs. noodles, cooked al dente

To make sauce, heat oil in saucepan. Sauté onion and garlic until golden. Stir in tomato sauce, water, basil, oregano, salt, sugar, pepper and parsley. Cover and simmer 10 minutes.

For veal, combine ½ cup parmesan cheese and ½ cup bread crumbs. Dip veal slices into beaten egg, then in cheese and bread crumb mixture. Heat 2 tablespoons oil in skillet and sauté veal until golden brown, turning only once. Repeat with remaining veal and oil.

Pour half the tomato mixture into a 9x13-inch baking dish. Lay mozzarella cheese over sauce., then veal. Continue to layer cheese and veal ending with cheese. Pour remaining sauce over top. Sprinkle with 3 tablespoons parmesan cheese. Bake at 350° for 25 minutes or until sauce is bubbly and cheese melts. Serve with noodles.

4-6 servings

reVeal your cooking talents

DAIRY LASAGNA

Show ■
Go □

Sauce:
1 c. chopped onions
1 clove garlic, crushed
¼ c. oil
2 (19 oz.) cans tomatoes
1 (6 oz.) can tomato paste
1 (8 oz.) can tomato sauce
2 T. chopped parsley
1 T. salt
1 T. sugar
1 T. oregano
1½ tsp. basil
1 T. pepper

Noodles:
1 (8 oz.) pkg. lasagna noodles,
    cooked

Filling:
2 lbs. dry cottage cheese
12 oz. shredded mozzarella cheese
2 eggs
½ c. grated parmesan cheese
1 T. chopped parsley
1 tsp. salt
¼ tsp. pepper

Topping:
grated parmesan cheese, to taste
4 oz. shredded mozzarella cheese

For sauce, sauté onions and garlic in oil. Add remaining sauce ingredients and simmer 1 hour. Combine filling ingredients. Pour layer of sauce into greased 10x14-inch pan to cover bottom. Add layer of cooked noodles and layer of filling, repeating layers of sauce, noodles and filling until all are used. Top with parmesan and mozzarella cheeses. Bake at 375° for 30 minutes.

12-16 servings

Healthy, "cheesey", & wise

LINGUINE WITH CLAM SAUCE

Show ■
Go ■

3 cloves garlic, crushed
¾ c. light olive oil
1 c. butter
2 doz. cherrystone clams, shucked or
    2 (7 ½ oz.) cans minced clams
½ c. finely chopped parsley
1 tsp. basil
½ tsp. oregano
crushed red pepper
freshly ground black pepper
1½ lbs. linguine, cooked al dente
grated parmesan cheese

Sauté garlic in oil and butter for 5 minutes. Add clams, parsley, basil, oregano and peppers. Simmer 20 minutes, stirring occasionally. Serve over linguine. Top with parmesan cheese.

4-6 servings

CHILES RELLENOS PIE

Show ■
Go ■

2 (4 oz.) cans mild green chiles, seeds
    removed
1 lb. shredded cheddar cheese
1 lb. shredded Monterey Jack cheese
¼ c. flour
1 (13 oz.) can evaporated milk
4 eggs
1 (8oz.) can tomato sauce

Line a 9x13-inch baking dish with chiles. Sprinkle with ⅓ of each cheese. Add another layer of chiles and ⅓ more cheese. Mix flour, milk and eggs in food processor or blender. Pour over cheeses. Sprinkle on remaining cheese. Bake at 375° for 30 minutes. Pour tomato sauce on top and bake 15 minutes longer. Can be frozen and reheated.

8-10 servings

MANICOTTI

Show ■
Go ☐

Sauce:
¼ c. olive oil
1 clove garlic, chopped
1 (28 oz.) can tomatoes with liquid
2 (6 oz.) cans tomato paste
2 T. chopped parsley
1 tsp. salt
1 T. sugar
½ c. chopped onion
¼ tsp. oregano
¼ tsp. basil
¼ tsp. pepper
2 T. butter

Filling:
¾ c. ricotta cheese
12 oz. mozzarella cheese, diced
½ c. grated parmesan cheese
3 eggs
1 tsp. salt
¼ tsp pepper
½ c. chopped parsley
½ c. grated parmesan cheese, for topping
1 (8 oz.) pkg. manicotti noodles, cooked,
    drained and cooled

Combine all ingredients for sauce and heat to boiling. Reduce heat and simmer one hour. In a large bowl, combine all filling ingredients except ½ cup parmesan cheese. Stuff manicotti with filling and place in greased 9x13-inch baking dish. Pour sauce over noodles and sprinkle with remaining parmesan cheese. Bake at 350° for 45 minutes.

6 servings

Sauce may be made ahead of time and refrigerated.

ITALIAN MAIN DISH PIE

Show ■
Go ■

1 (9-in.) unbaked frozen pie crust
   (or own recipe)
6 eggs
¼ c. milk
1 (7 oz.) can tuna, drained and flaked or
   1 c. flaked cooked fish
8 oz. shredded mozzarella cheese
¼ tsp. salt
¼ tsp. ground pepper
½ tsp. basil
½ tsp. oregano

Line a quiche pan with pastry, if not using prepared pie shell. Beat eggs and milk until blended. Add remaining ingredients and stir well. Spoon into crust. Bake at 425° for 35-40 minutes or until brown. Cut into wedges and serve hot.

6 servings

SPINACH QUICHE

Show ■
Go ■

1 (10 oz.) pkg. frozen chopped spinach,
   cooked and drained
8 oz. shredded cheddar cheese
4 oz. shredded mozzarella cheese
3 eggs, beaten
2 c. skim milk
1 (2.8 oz.) can French fried onion rings
¼ tsp. salt
¼ tsp. pepper
3-4 drops Tabasco

Mix cooled spinach with cheeses, eggs, milk, onions and spices. Pour into 9-inch quiche pan and bake at 350° for 40 minutes.

6-8 servings

HE-MAN quiche

BRUNCH EGG CASSEROLE

Show ■
Go ■

2 c. seasoned croutons
1½-2 c. shredded cheddar cheese
4 eggs, slightly beaten
2 c. milk
½ tsp. salt
½ tsp. dry mustard
⅛ tsp. onion powder
dash of pepper

Combine croutons and cheese in a greased 2 quart baking dish. Mix remaining ingredients in a large bowl with electric mixer until well blended. Pour egg mixture over croutons. Bake at 325° for 55-60 minutes or until golden brown.

6 servings

HOOTENANNY PANCAKE

Show ☐
Go ■

½ c. butter
6 eggs
1 c. milk
1 c. flour
½ tsp. salt
maple syrup or jam

Melt butter in a 9x13-inch glass baking dish. Beat eggs, milk, flour and salt together. Add to pan without stirring. Bake at 400° for 25-30 minutes. Cut in large squares and serve immediately. Top with maple syrup or jam.

4-6 servings

Also good with sliced apples, sautéed in butter and sprinkled with cinnamon-sugar mixture.

Serve a bunch for brunch!

APPLE KUCHEN

Show ■
Go ■

1 T. butter
1 c. flour
1 egg
½ tsp. baking powder
¼ c. sugar
2 T. milk
4-5 apples, peeled and sliced
2 T. sugar
1 tsp. cinnamon
1 egg yolk, beaten
3 T. heavy cream

Mix dry ingredients. Cut in butter with fingertips. Add milk and egg. Mix together. Toss onto lightly floured board. Pat or roll ¼ inch thick in a lightly greased 9x13-inch pan. Peel and cut apples. Lay apples parallel on top of dough. Sprinkle with sugar and cinnamon. Pour on beaten egg yolk. Drizzle cream on top of apples. Bake 350° for 20-30 minutes until apples are soft.

12 servings

BRUNCH FRENCH TOAST

Show ■
Go ☐

1 c. brown sugar
½ c. butter, melted
3 tsp. cinnamon, divided
3 tart apples, peeled and sliced
½ c. dried cranberries or raisins
1 loaf Italian or French bread, cut in
     1 inch slices
6 large eggs
1½ c. milk
1 T. vanilla

Place breadslices into a 9x13-inch pan. Combine brown sugar, butter and 1 tsp. cinnamon. Toss in apples and cranberries to coat well. Spread apple mixture evenly on top of bread. Mix eggs, milk, vanilla and remaining cinnamon. Pour over bread. Cover and refrigerate overnight. Cover with aluminum foil and bake in preheated 375° oven for 40 minutes. Uncover and bake another 5 minutes. Let stand 5 minutes. Serve warm.

12 servings

BIG APPLE PANCAKE

Show ■
Go ■

4 T. butter, divided
1 apple, peeled and sliced
½ c. milk
½ c. flour
4 large eggs, beaten
3 T. sugar
½ tsp. vanilla
¼ tsp. salt

Preheat oven to 450°. Grease a 9-inch glass pie pan. Sauté apples in 2 T. butter. When soft, place in prepared pie pan. Blend all ingredients except apples in blender or with a mixer. Pour slowly over sautéed apples. Bake about 15 minutes. Puffs up very tall. Lightly dust with powdered sugar, if desired. Serve immediately.

4 servings

VEGETABLE FRITTATA

Show ■
Go ☐

3 T. olive oil
1 lg. Spanish onion, thinly sliced
3 cloves fresh garlic, minced
2 med. summer squash, sliced ¼ inch
    thick then sliced in half
2 med. zucchini, sliced ¼ inch thick
    then sliced in half
1 red bell pepper, seeded and cut
    into ¼ inch wide strips
1 yellow bell pepper, seeded and cut
    into ¼ inch wide strips
1 green bell pepper, seeded and cut
    into ¼ inch wide strips
8 oz. fresh mushrooms, sliced
6 lg. eggs
¼ c. heavy whipping cream
2 tsp. salt
2 tsp freshly ground pepper
2 c. stale French bread cubes (½ inch
    pieces)
8 oz. cream cheese, cut into small pieces
2 c. grated Swiss cheese

Preheat oven to 350°. Grease the bottom and sides of a 10-inch springform pan. Heat oil in large pan over medium high heat. Add onion, garlic, summer squash, zucchini, peppers and mushrooms. Sauté for 15-20 minutes until vegetables are tender crisp. Drain juices. Whisk the eggs and cream together in a large mixing bowl. Season with salt and pepper. Stir in bread, cream cheese and Swiss cheese. Add the sautéed vegetables to egg mixture and stir until well combined. Pour into prepared pan and pack mixture tightly. Place pan on a baking sheet to catch any leaks. Bake frittata about 1 hour and 10 minutes until firm to the touch, puffed and golden brown. If the top is getting too brown, cover with aluminum foil. Serve hot or cold.

8 servings

Side Dishes

ISRAELI SKILLET EGGPLANT

Show ■
Go ■

1 med. eggplant, skin on
1 med. onion, peeled
1 med. green pepper
2 tomatoes, peeled
¼ c. oil
1 clove garlic, chopped
2 tsp. salt
½ tsp. pepper

Cut eggplant, onion, green pepper and tomatoes into chunks. Heat oil, garlic, salt and pepper in skillet. Add vegetables except tomatoes, cover and simmer, stirring occasionally about 12-14 minutes or until tender. Add tomatoes last 5 minutes. Serve immediately or place in casserole and keep warm in 300° degree oven.

4-6 servings

May top with parmesan or shredded mozzarella cheese before baking.

MOM'S LIMA BEANS

Show ■
Go ■

6 (15½ oz.) cans butter beans
¾ c. brown sugar, packed
¼ c. tomato soup, undiluted
1 c. ketchup
½ c. whipping cream
1 tsp. dry mustard
6 T. butter, softened
salt and pepper to taste

Drain beans well and place in 3-quart casserole; mix in remaining ingredients. Bake uncovered at 375° degrees for 45-50 minutes.

18-20 servings

Mama knows best!

SPINACH SQUARES

Show ■
Go ■

2 (10 oz.) pkgs. frozen spinach, cooked
    and drained
¼ c. flour
1 tsp. salt
¼ tsp. pepper
6 eggs, well beaten
1 (24 oz.) carton large curd cottage cheese
12 oz. shredded sharp cheddar cheese
¼ c. bread crumbs

Mix spinach well with flour, salt and pepper; add eggs, cottage cheese and cheddar cheese. Place in greased 9x13-inch glass baking dish; top with bread crumbs. Bake at 350° for 45 minutes. Remove from oven and let stand a few minutes before cutting.

10-12 servings

May be frozen after baking; defrost and heat.

SPINACH ROLL WITH MUSHROOM SAUCE

Show ■
Go ■

2 (10 oz.) pkgs. frozen chopped spinach,
    thawed and drained
2 eggs
1 envelope dry onion soup mix
⅔ c. Ricotta cheese
Mushroom Sauce (see index)

Blend spinach, eggs and onion soup mix in a blender or food processor. Spread on a greased 10½x15½-inch jelly roll pan or cookie sheet. Square edges to form a 9x13-inch rectangle. Bake at 350° for 20 minutes. Gently release from pan. Whip Ricotta cheese and spread over baked spinach. Starting at narrow end, roll up like a jelly roll. Heat at 350° for 10 minutes or until hot. Serve with Mushroom Sauce.

6 servings

SIMPLE SPINACH SOUFFLE

Show ■
Go ■

½ onion, chopped
1 T. butter
1¼ T. flour
1 (10 oz.) pkg. frozen chopped spinach,
    cooked and drained
1 c. cottage cheese
3 eggs, beaten well
salt
pepper
grated parmesan cheese
nutmeg

Sauté onion in melted butter, add flour and spinach. Mix in cottage cheese, eggs, salt and pepper. Place in buttered 1½-quart casserole. Sprinkle with parmesan cheese and nutmeg and set in pan of hot water. Bake uncovered at 350° for 1 hour.

6-8 servings

LAYERED VEGETABLE SOUFFLE

Show ■
Go ■

2-3 (12 oz.) pkgs. frozen Stouffer's
    Spinach Souffle
2-3 (12 oz.) pkgs. frozen Stouffer's
    Corn Souffle
1 (16 oz.) pkg. frozen sliced or baby
    carrots
2 T. butter (optional)
2 T. brown sugar (optional)

Place frozen layer of each vegetable in 9x13-inch baking dish. Dot with butter and sprinkle with brown sugar, if desired. Bake uncovered at 350° for 1 hour or until puffy. Serve immediately.

10-12 servings

May omit brown sugar and sprinkle with parmesan cheese.

So easy it's embarrassing!

CARROT BROCCOLI SUPREME

Show ■
Go ■

1½ c. sliced carrots
1 med. onion, sliced
1 (10 oz.) pkg. frozen broccoli
3 T. butter
3 T. flour
1½ c. milk
1 c. shredded sharp cheddar cheese
4 tsp. salt
dash each pepper, dry mustard, cayenne
  and Worcestershire
1 (2.8 oz.) can French fried onion rings

Cook carrots and onion until tender. Set aside. Cook and drain broccoli. In a separate saucepan melt butter; remove from heat and add flour gradually. Return to heat, add milk, stirring constantly until mixture thickens. Add cheese and spices. Grease an 8x8-inch pan and layer broccoli, carrots, onion and sauce, ending with sauce. Bake at 350° for 45 minutes. Sprinkle onion rings on top and bake for 15 minutes more.

6 servings

Recipe may be doubled in a 9x13-inch pan

ZUCCHINI SOUFFLE

Show ■
Go ■

½ tsp. salt
6 c. grated zucchini
1 med. onion, sliced
2 T. butter
4 eggs
¼ c. milk
¾ c. bread crumbs
½ tsp. basil
½ tsp. oregano
1 c. shredded mozzarella cheese

Sprinkle salt over zucchini in large bowl and let rest for 10 minutes. Sauté onion in butter. Squeeze excess water from zucchini and add onion. Beat eggs and milk slightly and mix with zucchini. Add bread crumbs and spices. Pour into a greased 2 quart souffle dish and bake at 400° for 30 minutes. Cover with cheese and bake another 10 minutes or until knife inserted in center comes out clean. Serve immediately.

8-10 servings

BAKED ZUCCHINI

Show ■
Go ■

4 c. chopped zucchini
1 c. Bisquick
4 eggs, slightly beaten
½ c. oil
1 onion, finely chopped
1 c. shredded Monterey Jack cheese
1 tsp. cinnamon
1 T. chopped parsley
salt
pepper

Mix all ingredients together in one bowl. Put in 3 quart buttered casserole. Bake at 350° for 30 minutes. Let stand 10 minutes.

6-8 servings

ZUCCHINI CUSTARD

Show ■
Go ■

4 lg. zucchini, sliced
1 egg
½ c. dairy sour cream
¾ tsp. Jane's Krazy Mixed-up Salt
¼ tsp. pepper
1 c. freshly grated parmesan cheese
2 T. butter

Cook zucchini, covered in salted, boiling water until tender. Drain well. Place in shallow baking dish or quiche pan. Mix egg, sour cream, salt, pepper and ½ cup cheese together by hand. Pour over zucchini. Dot with butter and remaining cheese. Bake at 400° for 15 minutes.

6 servings

When doubling recipe, double baking time.

Zucchini's last stand!

ROADSIDE POTATOES

Show ■
Go ■

1 (32 oz.) pkg. frozen hash brown potatoes, thawed
½ c. butter, melted
1 c. shredded cheddar cheese
1 c. grated parmesan cheese
¾ c. half and half cream
1 med. onion, grated
salt
pepper
paprika
6 T. butter

Combine potatoes, melted butter, cheeses, cream, onion, salt and pepper. Spread mixture in 9x13-inch well greased baking dish. Sprinkle with paprika; dot with butter. Bake at 350° for 1½ hours.

8-10 servings

The mixture can also be baked in greased muffin tins for only 45-50 minutes. Let stand one minute before removing from pan. 30 muffins

AU GRATIN POTATOES

Show ■
Go ■

1 sm. onion, finely chopped
1 (32 oz.) pkg. frozen hash brown potatoes, thawed
1 (10½ oz.) can cream of mushroom soup
12 oz. dairy sour cream
12 oz. shredded cheddar cheese
¾ c. corn flakes
¼ c. butter, melted

Mix onion, potatoes, soup, sour cream and cheese together and place in a greased 9x13-inch baking dish. Sprinkle with corn flakes and melted butter. Bake at 350° for 1¼ hours.

8-10 servings

Enjoy! Enjoy!

PARMESAN POTATOES

Show ■
Go ■

½ c. unsalted butter
parmesan cheese
5 med. potatoes, scrubbed
garlic salt
seasoned salt
paprika

Melt butter in foil-lined 10½ x 15½ -inch jelly roll pan. Sprinkle a thin layer of parmesan cheese over butter. Cut potatoes in half lengthwise and place in pan, skin side up. Season with salts and paprika. Spoon some of the butter over top and add more seasoning. Bake uncovered at 350° for 1-1½ hours or until crispy.

5-10 servings

DOUBLE CREAM MASHED POTATOES

Show ■
Go ■

9 lg. potatoes, peeled and boiled
2 (3 oz.) pkgs. cream cheese, softened
2 tsp. onion salt
1 tsp. salt
¼ tsp. pepper
2 T. butter or margarine
1 c. dairy sour cream
1 T. butter
paprika

Mash potatoes and beat together with cream cheese, salts, pepper, 2 tablespoons butter and sour cream. Spread in a greased 9x13 -inch pan. Cover and refrigerate several hours or overnight. Dot with remaining butter and sprinkle with paprika. Bake at 350° for 30 minutes.

8-10 servings

Throw calories to the wind!

ONION CASSEROLE

Show ■
Go ☐

¼ c. unsalted butter
7-8 lg. onions, cut into chunks
½ c. uncooked rice
1 tsp. salt
5 c. water
1 c. grated Jarlsberg or Swiss cheese
⅔ c. half and half cream
salt

In large skillet, melt butter over medium heat and sauté onions until transparent. Remove from heat. Cook rice in boiling, salted water 5 minutes. Drain well. Add rice, cheese and cream to onions and mix well. Salt to taste. Place mixture in greased 2-quart shallow casserole. Bake at 325° for 1 hour. May be served hot or cold.

6-8 servings

VEGETABLE KASHA CASSEROLE

Show ■
Go ■

1½ c. kasha
3 eggs
1 envelope dry onion soup mix
3 c. water
1 (16 oz.) pkg. frozen or fresh mixed
    vegetables
1 T. butter
salt
pepper
1 (10½ oz.) can cream of mushroom soup

Mix kasha and 1 egg in pan and heat for 1 or 2 minutes, stirring constantly. Remove from heat. Boil onion soup in water for 5-10 minutes. Add soup to kasha and cover pan tightly for 8-10 minutes until kasha is tender. Cook vegetables 5-8 minutes until they are crisp and tender. Butter and season to taste. Beat remaining eggs and add to vegetables. Butter a 2 quart casserole and put in ½ of the kasha mixture. Put vegetables on top. Add mushroom soup to remaining kasha and spread on top of casserole. Bake at 350° for 1 hour.

8-10 servings

MUSHROOM STRUDEL

Show ■
Go ☐

2 lbs. fresh mushrooms, minced
1 c. minced onion
8 shallots, minced
4-6 T. butter
2 T. oil
1 c. dairy sour cream
¼ c. minced fresh dill weed
salt and pepper
28 fillo strudel leaves
¾ to 1 c. butter, melted

Place mushrooms in towel, a handful at a time and squeeze out moisture. Sauté onion and shallots in skillet in butter and oil until all moisture is evaporated. Add sour cream, dill weed, salt and pepper. (If filling seems too thin, add a little flour to thicken.)

For each roll, place 1 fillo leaf on waxed paper. Brush well with butter. Repeat until 7 leaves are stacked and buttered. Keep remaining leaves covered with damp towel.

Spread a 1 inch wide strip of mushroom filling on long side of buttered fillo leaf. Fold in sides and roll up. Transfer roll to greased cookie sheet and place seam side down. Brush with melted butter. Repeat with other 3 rolls. Bake at 350° for 45 minutes or until crisp and golden. Cool 5 minutes. Cut diagonal slices 1 inch thick and serve warm.

36 slices

To freeze: Place unbaked on cookie sheet; when frozen, wrap individually and return to freezer. Also makes a nice appetizer.

Cave in on this one!

MUSHROOM RICE MOLD

Show ■
Go ■

1 c. uncooked rice
8 oz. fresh mushrooms, sliced
1-2 cloves garlic, crushed
2-3 onions, finely chopped
¼ c. butter
salt
pepper

Cook rice as directed on package. Sauté mushrooms, garlic and onions in butter until soft but not overcooked. Add vegetables to rice and season to taste. Mix well and place in 6½-cup ring mold. Bake at 350° for 30 minutes. Invert on serving plate. Fill center with your favorite cooked vegetable.

6-8 servings

BROWN RICE STRUDEL

Show ■
Go ☐

1½ c. uncooked brown rice
3 c. boiling water
1 c. chopped onions
1 c. chopped fresh mushrooms
2 T. butter
2 T. sesame seeds
3 c. shredded cheddar cheese
1 tsp. salt
½ tsp. white pepper
½ c. butter, softened
10 fillo strudel leaves
melted butter
sesame seeds

Cook rice in water for 1 hour. Let cool. Sauté onions and mushrooms in butter until tender. Add sesame seeds and cook another minute. Add to rice and shredded cheese, salt and pepper. Cool mixture thoroughly.

Butter and stack 5 fillo leaves; place ½ of filling mixture on narrow end of fillo leaves and roll up. Slash top in 5 places, brush with melted butter and sprinkle with sesame seeds. Repeat for second roll. Cover with plastic wrap and refrigerate until butter is firm or until ready to use. Rolls may be frozen or refrigerated until the next day

Place on greased cookie sheet. Bake at 350° for 30 minutes. (If frozen, partially thaw before baking.) Cut each roll in 6 pieces for side dish or larger for main course.

12 servings

ALMOND FRIED RICE

Show ■
Go ■

1½ c. uncooked rice
¼ c. salad oil
⅔ c. chopped green onion
⅔ c. chopped green pepper
1 clove garlic, finely chopped
1 tsp. salt
¼ tsp. black pepper
½ c. soy sauce
1 c. sliced almonds

Cook rice as directed on package. In large skillet, heat oil; sauté onion, green pepper, garlic, salt and pepper until lightly browned. Add rice, soy sauce and almonds. Sauté 10 minutes, stirring lightly as it cooks.

6 servings

GREEN RICE

Show ■
Go ■

1 c. plus 1 T. uncooked rice
2-3 T. chicken broth
½ c. butter
1 med. green pepper
4 green onions
2½ T. chopped fresh parsley
1 tsp. salt

Cook rice as directed on package, adding chicken broth to water. Cool and place in large mixing bowl. Melt butter; add to rice and set aside. In blender or food processor, chop green pepper and onions, add to rice with parsley and salt. Pour into a lightly greased 4½ cup mold. Cover and bake at 350° for 1 hour.

8-10 servings

This is great with pepper steak or any chicken dish.

Holiday on rice!

FILLO DE ESPINARDS

Show ■
Go ☐

2 lbs. fresh spinach, washed or 2 (10 oz.)
    pkgs. frozen spinach
8 oz. shredded mozzarella cheese
1 c. freshly grated parmesan cheese
¼ c. cold butter, cut into small pieces
salt and pepper to taste
cinnamon, 3 good shakes
½ c. finely chopped green onions
1 c. unsalted butter, melted
1 pkg. fillo strudel leaves
bread crumbs
finely chopped parsley

If using fresh spinach, place in boiling water for a few minutes. Drain well. Remove stems and chop leaves finely. If using frozen spinach, thaw and drain completely. Add cheeses, ¼ cup butter, salt, pepper, cinnamon and onions. Mix thoroughly.

Brush with butter and stack 6 fillo leaves, sprinkling bread crumbs on each leaf. Place ⅓ of filling mixture on long ends of leaves. Roll up, jelly roll fashion, folding in ends. Place on greased cookie sheet, seam side down. Brush with melted butter and sprinkle with parsley. Repeat for 2 more rolls.

Bake at 400° for 15 minutes. Remove from oven, cut with serrated knife into serving portions. Return to oven and bake 10 minutes or until golden brown.

8-10 servings

May be assembled the day before and baked just before serving. To freeze: Prepare to baking stage and wrap tightly. Thaw before baking.

STRAW AND HAY

Show ■
Go ☐

2 T. butter
¾ lb. fresh mushrooms, thickly sliced
salt and pepper
½ c. whipping cream or half and half
½-¾ lb. egg fettuccine
½-¾ lb. spinach fettuccine
2 T. Pesto Sauce (see index)
2 T. butter
⅓ c. chicken stock, heated
1 c. whipping cream or half and half
freshly grated parmesan cheese

In large skillet melt 2 tablespoons butter and sauté mushrooms until tender. Season to taste with salt and pepper. Add ½ cup cream and cook until cream thickens slightly. Set aside. Cook both fettuccines al dente. Drain and return to large pot. Stir in Pesto Sauce and 2 tablespoons butter, and mix until melted. Add chicken stock and toss to moisten. Add 1 cup cream and cook gently until sauce thickens slightly. Add mushroom-cream mixture. Taste and correct seasoning. Serve freshly grated parmesan cheese on the side.

12 servings

NOODLES FLORENTINE

Show ■
Go ■

1 (10 oz.) pkg. broad noodles
1 (10½ oz.) can cream of mushroom soup
½ soup can milk
¾ c. shredded cheddar cheese
2 (12 oz.) pkgs. frozen spinach souffle,
    thawed
½ c. butter
bread crumbs
¼ c. shredded cheddar cheese

Cook and drain noodles. Mix mushroom soup, milk and ¾ cup cheese and add to noodles. Fold in spinach souffle and pour into 1½ quart greased casserole. Melt butter and combine with bread crumbs. Mix ¼ cup cheese with buttered bread crumbs and sprinkle over top of casserole. Bake at 350° for 1 hour.

6 servings

BLUE HORSE FETTUCCINE ALFREDO

Show ■
Go ■

1 lb. fettuccine
2 T. butter
1 c. whipping cream
2 egg yolks
pinch of salt
freshly ground pepper to taste
¼ c. grated parmesan cheese

Cook fettuccine al dente in rapidly boiling salted water. Drain well and toss in pan over low heat until quite dry. Add butter, cream, egg yolks, salt and pepper and mix well. When hot, add parmesan cheese and continue tossing lightly until well blended. Place on individual plates, sprinkle lightly with more parmesan cheese and serve immediately.

4-6 servings

SPINACH FETTUCCINE

Show ■
Go ■

1 lb. fresh spinach or 1 (10 oz.) pkg.
    frozen spinach
2 cloves garlic, chopped
2 T. chopped pignoli (pine nuts)
½ c. chopped walnuts
½ c. Ricotta cheese
½ c. grated parmesan cheese
¼ tsp. ginger
¼ tsp. nutmeg
1 lb. fettuccine
½ c. butter
1 c. whipping cream
nutmeg and walnut pieces for garnish

Cook spinach and drain well. In a large bowl, mix garlic and nuts with cheeses and spices. Cook fettuccine al dente. Drain and return to saucepan. Add butter and cream and cook over high heat. Stir in cheese mixture and toss well. Serve hot. Garnish with nutmeg and walnut pieces.

4-6 servings

PASTA PRIMAVERA

Show ■
Go ☐

1 lb. fresh broccoli
1 med. zucchini
½ lb. fresh asparagus
1 lb. linguine noodles
1 clove garlic, finely chopped
1 pt. cherry tomatoes, halved
¼ c. olive oil
¼ c. chopped fresh basil
½ lb. fresh mushrooms, sliced
¼ c. chopped fresh parsley
1½ tsp. salt
¼ tsp. pepper
¼ tsp. crushed red pepper
¼ c. butter
¾ c. whipping cream
⅔ c. grated parmesan cheese

Wash and trim broccoli, zucchini and asparagus. Cut into bite-size pieces. Cook in salted boiling water. Cook and drain linguine, set both aside in large bowls. Sauté garlic and tomatoes in oil for 2 minutes. Stir in basil and mushrooms. Cook 3 minutes. Add parsley, salt and peppers. Cook 1 more minute. Add mixture to vegetables. Melt butter in separate pan. Add cream and cheese. Cook over low heat, stirring constantly until smooth. Add cooked linguine. Toss to coat. Stir in vegetables and heat gently until hot.

8-10 servings

Do not overcook vegetables.

pasta to lasta lifetime

INDIVIDUAL NOODLE KUGELS

Show ■
Go □

1 (8 oz.) pkg. med. noodles
⅓ c. butter, softened
2 eggs
1 T. sugar
3 T. brown sugar
1 tsp. cinnamon
¼ c. golden raisins
15 dried apricots, finely cut up
8 tsp. butter
16 walnut halves
16 tsp. brown sugar

Cook and drain noodles. In mixer, combine butter, eggs, sugar, 3 tablespoons brown sugar, cinnamon, raisins and apricots. Mix with noodles in a large bowl. Grease muffin tins well and place ½ tsp. butter in bottom of each cup. Place walnut half upside down on top of the butter and 1 tsp. of brown sugar on top of the walnut. Pat noodles firmly into each cup on top of the butter, nut and brown sugar. Bake at 350° for 15-20 minutes. Watch carefully. Remove from oven and let stand 5 minutes. With a knife, loosen edges of noodle puddings. Invert and serve.

16 kugels

These freeze beautifully. To reheat, place thawed noodle puddings on cookie sheet and heat at 325° for 10 minutes or until hot.

NOODLE KUGEL WITH LEMON SAUCE

Show ■
Go ☐

½ c. butter
8 oz. wide noodles, cooked and drained
8 oz. cream cheese, softened
¾ c. sugar
4 eggs
1 c. milk
dash of salt
1 tsp. vanilla
½ c. golden raisins (optional)

Topping:
1 c. crushed corn or bran flakes
¼ c. cinnamon-sugar

Lemon sauce:
½-¾ c. lemon juice
1½ c. water
3 eggs, separated
1 c. sugar
2½ T. cornstarch
¼ c. cold water

Place butter on cooked noodles to melt. Whip cream cheese and sugar; add eggs (1 at a time), milk, salt and vanilla in blender or food processor. Add raisins if desired. Combine with noodles and spread in greased 9x13-inch pan. Top with crushed flakes and cinnamon-sugar. Bake at 350° for 1 hour or until top is golden brown.

For lemon sauce, combine lemon juice, water, egg yolks, sugar and cornstarch that has been dissolved in cold water. Cook over low heat, stirring constantly until thick and smooth. Beat egg whites until stiff and fold by hand into completely cooled sauce. Refrigerate until needed.

12-14 servings

Even great without the lemon sauce.

a treasured recipe

CHEESE AND SPINACH PIE

Show ☐
Go ■

1 (10 oz.) pkg. frozen chopped spinach,
cooked and drained
1 lb. Ricotta cheese
1 c. shredded mozzarella, Feta or cheddar
cheese (or a combination)
3 eggs, slightly beaten
2 T. oil
½ tsp. onion salt
½ tsp. garlic salt
½ tsp. freshly ground pepper
10-inch frozen deep-dish pie crust
2 T. butter

Combine cooled spinach with cheeses, eggs, oil and seasonings. Pour into pie crust; dot with butter. Bake at 350° for 40 minutes.

8 servings

May add sliced mushrooms, zucchini and green pepper if desired and bake in larger pie plate. Also may be made without crust.

MORE THAN A SPINACH RING

Show ■
Go ■

2 (10 oz.) pkgs. frozen chopped spinach,
thawed and drained
1 lg. onion, chopped
¼ c. butter
½ lb. wide egg noodles
¼ lb. narrow egg noodles
16 oz. dairy sour cream
6 eggs, beaten
salt and pepper (needs a lot)

Press all water out of spinach. Sauté onion in butter until transparent. Cook noodles together in boiling water. Drain and let cool. Add to spinach and mix in sour cream, eggs, salt and pepper. Spoon into a greased 6½-cup ring mold; place in pan of hot water. Bake at 350° for 1 hour.

6-8 servings

THE ORIGINAL CARROT RING

Show ■
Go ■

2¼ c. Vegetable Shortening
1½ c. brown sugar
3 eggs, separated
3 c. flour
3 tsp. baking powder
1½ tsp. baking soda
1½ tsp. salt
3 T. water
1 T. lemon juice
3 c. shredded carrots

Cream Vegetable Shortening and brown sugar together by hand. Add egg yolks and mix well. Mix flour, baking powder, soda and salt. Add to mixture alternately with water and lemon juice that has been mixed together. Add shredded carrots. Beat egg whites and fold into the mixture. Pour into 15 cup greased ring mold or springform pan. Bake at 350° for 45-60 minutes.

12-14 servings

PUMPKIN MOLD

Show ■
Go ■

1½ c. flour
1⅓ c. sugar
¼ tsp. baking powder
1 tsp. baking soda
¾ tsp. salt
1 tsp. cinnamon
¼ tsp. nutmeg
⅓ c. shortening
⅓ c. chopped nuts
⅓ c. water
⅔ c. raisins
1 c. canned pumpkin
1 egg

Sift dry ingredients together into a large bowl. Add remaining ingredients and mix well. Pour into greased 6-cup ring mold. Bake at 350° for 45 minutes. Let stand 15 minutes before unmolding.

6-8 servings

May double the recipe and bake in a bundt pan.

Break the common mold

MAPLE GLAZED CARROTS

Show ■
Go ■

4½ c. water
4 lbs. carrots, peeled and cut on the
    diagonal into ¼-inch ovals
    (about 11 cups)
1¼ sticks unsalted butter
3 T. sugar
1½ tsp kosher salt
6 T. pure maple syrup
3 T. dark brown sugar, packed
2 T. Italian parsley, chopped

Combine water, carrots, 4T. butter, sugar and salt in large, heavy pot. Bring to a boil. Reduce heat, cover and simmer 10 minutes until carrots are tender when pierced with a knife. Melt remaining butter in a large non-stick skillet over medium heat. Add maple syrup and brown sugar and stir until sugar is dissolved. Add carrots and cook 5 minutes until heated through. Season with salt and pepper. Transfer to a serving bowl and sprinkle with parsley.

8 servings

SCALLOPED SWEET POTATOES WITH PRALINE TOPPING

Show ■
Go ■

¼ c. brown sugar, packed
3 T. butter, room temperature
3 T. flour
⅓ c. pecans, finely chopped
6 medium sweet potatoes, peeled and cut
    into ½-inch thick rounds
2 c. heavy whipping cream, heated

In a small bowl mix brown sugar, butter and flour. Add pecans. Set aside. Bring a large pot of lightly salted water to a boil. Add sweet potatoes. Cook until fork-tender, about 5 minutes. Do not overcook. Drain and rinse under cold running water. Preheat oven to 375°. Lightly butter a 9x13-inch baking dish. Arrange sweet potatoes in vertical rows overlapping edges and cover with warm cream. Bake for 20 minutes. Sprinkle with pecan mixture. Continue baking for 20-30 minutes until sweet potatoes are tender and topping is browned.

8-12 servings

GRATIN OF BUTTERNUT SQUASH

Show ■
Go ☐

12 slices butternut squash
oive oil
6 oz. heavy cream
6 oz. aged Goat cheese
½ c. sliced leeks, sautéed
salt to taste

Cut off the top of the butternut squash. Peel and slice into ½ inch pieces. Place squash on parchment paper on a jelly roll pan and brush with olive oil. Bake at 325° for 20 minutes until squash is fork tender. Grease a 9x13-inch casserole and line with 6 pieces of squash. Drizzle with cream and place a dollop of Goat cheese over each piece. Sprinkle with sautéed leeks. Season with salt and repeat with a second layer. Bake at 400° for 8 minutes or until cheese is lightly browned.

8-10 servings

OVEN ROASTED VEGETABLES

Show ■
Go ■

10 unpeeled whole small new potatoes, quartered
1 c. baby carrots, peeled
1 small onion, cut into wedges
¼ c. olive oil
2 T. lemon juice
1 T. balsamic vinegar
3 cloves garlic, minced
1 T. fresh rosemary or oregano
1 tsp. salt
½ tsp. pepper
½ small eggplant, quartered lengthwise and cut into 2 inch slices
1 medium red or green pepper, cut into ⅓ inch strips

Combine potatoes, carrots and onions in a 9x13-inch baking pan. In a small mixing bowl, combine olive oil, lemon juice, garlic, rosemary or oregano, salt and pepper. Drizzle over vegetables in baking pan. Toss to coat. Roast uncovered at 450° for 30 minutes, stirring occasionally. Remove from oven. Add eggplant and red or green pepper. Toss to combine. Return to oven and roast 15-20 minutes until vegetables are tender and brown on edges.

6-8 servings

POTATO GRATIN WITH BOURSIN CHEESE

Show ■
Go ■

2 c. whipping cream
5 oz. Boursin cheese with herbs
3 lbs. red potatoes, unpeeled and
    uncooked, thinly sliced (¼-inch rounds)
1½ T. fresh, chopped parsley

Preheat oven to 400°. Butter a 9x13-inch baking dish. In a saucepan, heat whipping cream and cheese over low heat stirring until smooth. Layer the baking dish with ½ the potatoes and ½ of the sauce, repeat. Bake for one hour, uncovered. Sprinkle with chopped parsley.

8 servings

Holiday Fare

THANKSGIVING BREAD STUFFING

Show ■
Go ☐

1 challah bread
1 lb. seasoned bread cubes
4 c. chopped celery
4 c. chopped onion
1 c. butter
¼ c. chicken fat
1 c. butter, melted
3 eggs, beaten
3 c. warm water
4 lg. potatoes, peeled and shredded
2 tsp. poultry seasoning
2 tsp. sage
1 tsp. each celery salt, thyme, salt
    and pepper

Dry challah by leaving it out uncovered overnight. Break it in small pieces and mix with bread cubes. Sauté celery and onion in 1 cup butter and add to bread mixture. Add remaining ingredients. Stuff the bird loosely with this moist mixture.

Place extra stuffing in a casserole and bake covered at 325° for 2 hours.

Stuffing for 1 large turkey plus extra casserole

6-8 servings

CHOCOLATE CHIP MANDEL BROT

Show ■
Go ☐

½ c. butter or margarine
1 c. sugar
2 eggs
1 tsp. vanilla
1 tsp. almond extract
2 c. flour
1 tsp. baking powder
¼ tsp. cinnamon
½ c. chocolate chips
¼ c. sugar
½ tsp. cinnamon

Cream butter and sugar. Add eggs, vanilla and almond extract. Stir flour, baking powder and cinnamon into creamed mixture. Add chocolate chips and mix well. Using wet hands, divide dough into 3 parts. Make a loaf out of each and place on greased cookie sheet, leaving a few inches between each loaf. Bake at 350° for 25-30 minutes. Remove from oven and slice each loaf in 6-8 pieces. Combine remaining sugar and cinnamon; sprinkle on slices. Return to oven and bake 5-10 minutes longer. Cool.

18-24 pieces

FROZEN PUMPKIN ICE CREAM PIE

Show ■
Go ☐

Crust:
¾ c. whole pitted dates
¼ c. water
¼ c. butter or margarine
1½ c. crushed corn flakes
1 T. sugar
⅓ c. chopped pecans

Filling:
1 pt. vanilla ice cream, softened
1 c. canned pumpkin
1¼ c. sugar
½ tsp. salt
¼ tsp. nutmeg
½ tsp. ginger
½ tsp. cinnamon
1 c. whipping cream

For crust, place dates and water in saucepan; cook over low heat, stirring frequently until paste is formed. Add butter, blend and cook until melted. Remove from heat; add corn flakes, sugar and nuts. Blend well. Press into bottom and side of 9-inch pie plate, using back of tablespoon.

For filling, line side of crust with ice cream. Blend together the pumpkin, sugar, salt, nutmeg, ginger and cinnamon. Whip and fold in cream and place mixture in crust and freeze at least 4 hours. Remove from freezer 15 minutes before serving. Garnish with additional whipped cream, if desired.

8-10 servings

HOLIDAY HONEY CAKE

Show ■
Go ☐

3 eggs
1 c. sugar
2 tsp. baking soda
¾ c. cold coffee
1 c. honey
1 c. apricot preserves
¾ c. oil
1 tsp. cinnamon
1 tsp. allspice
½ tsp. salt
1 c. chopped nuts
juice and grated rind of 1 orange
1 apple, shredded with peel
3 c. flour

In large mixing bowl, cream eggs and sugar. Dissolve soda in coffee. Add honey, preserves, oil, spices, salt, nuts and coffee mixture to creamed mixture. Blend well. Add orange juice, rind and apple. Stir in flour and mix well. Line with waxed paper and grease a 15x4x4-inch or two 5x9-inch plus 1 mini size loaf pan and pour in mixture. Bake at 325° for 40 minutes, then increase oven to 350° and bake 20 minutes or until toothpick comes out clean. Let stand for a while before inverting pan. Remove waxed paper.

25 servings

CHAROSES FOR PASSOVER

Show ■
Go ■

¼ c. raisins
½ c. sherry
1 c. peeled, finely chopped apple
1 lg. banana, cut in bite-size pieces
¼ c. coarsely chopped walnuts
¼ c. chopped dates (optional)
1 tsp. honey
1 tsp. cinnamon
1-2 T. sweet red wine

Soak raisins in sherry overnight; refrigerate. When ready to use, drain and add remaining ingredients by hand.

2 cups

MOCK KISHKA FOR PASSOVER

Show ■
Go ■

1 (10 oz.) box egg matzo crackers
2 lg. carrots
3 ribs celery
1 lg. onion
2 eggs
¼ c. butter or margarine, melted
salt and pepper

Crush crackers in food processor. Empty bowl and finely chop all vegetables. Add butter and eggs; process until blended. Add crackers, salt and pepper and blend well. Form 2 rolls about 1½ inches in diameter and wrap tightly in foil. May be prepared in advance to this point and refrigerated or frozen until needed. (Thaw before baking.) Bake in foil on cookie sheet at 350° for 45-50 minutes. Remove foil and slice in 2 inch slices.

16 slices

MATZO STUFFING

Show ■
Go ■

¾ c. minced onion
1½ c. coarsely chopped almonds
¼ lb. fresh mushrooms, sliced
¾ c. vegetable shortening
10 matzos, finely broken or 7 c.
    matzo farfel
1 tsp. salt
¼ tsp. pepper
1 T. paprika
1 egg, beaten
2 c. clear chicken soup

Sauté onion, almonds and mushrooms in shortening until tender but not brown. Add matzos and cook 1 minute. Combine salt, pepper, paprika, egg and soup. Add to matzo mixture and mix well.

Stuffing for a 10-12 pound turkey

PASSOVER APPLE KUGEL

Show ■
Go ■

6 matzos
4 apples, peeled and cut into eighths
1½ c. raisins
½ tsp. cinnamon
rind of ½ lemon, grated
4-6 T. orange juice
1 c. sugar
¼ c. butter, melted
6 eggs, well beaten

Soak matzos in cold water until soft. Drain off water in colander. Combine matzos, apples, raisins, cinnamon, lemon rind, orange juice, sugar and butter. Add eggs; blend well. Pour into greased 9x13-inch pan. Bake at 350° for 30-40 minutes.

16 servings

A rash of holiday ideas

PASSOVER ONION KUGEL

Show ■
Go ■

6 eggs, separated
2 c. finely chopped onions
⅓ c. peanut oil
⅓ c. matzo meal
1-1½ tsp. salt
¼ tsp. pepper

Grease a 2 quart casserole and place in 350° oven a few minutes to heat. Beat egg yolks until thick and creamy. Add onions, oil, matzo meal, salt and pepper; mix well. Beat egg whites until stiff. Fold into onion mixture, pour into casserole. Bake at 350° for 30 minutes or until knife inserted in center comes out clean.

6 servings

SPINACH FRITTATA FOR PASSOVER

Show ■
Go ■

2 (10 oz.) pkgs. frozen chopped spinach,
    thawed and drained
6 eggs, beaten
1 c. grated parmesan cheese
½ c. crumbled Feta cheese (or any
    mild cheese)
1 c. cottage cheese
¼ c. oil
⅓ c. matzo meal
¼ c. grated parmesan cheese
yogurt or dairy sour cream

Place spinach in large mixing bowl. Add eggs and blend well. Add parmesan, Feta and cottage cheese, oil and matzo meal, mixing thoroughly. Pour into greased 9x13-inch baking dish. Sprinkle with ¼ cup parmesan cheese. Bake at 350° for 1 hour. Cool slightly and cut into squares. Serve warm with yogurt or sour cream.

16 servings

May omit Feta cheese and just add ½ cup additional cottage cheese.

PASSOVER APPLE CARROT CASSEROLE

Show ■
Go ■

3 eggs, separated
½ c. butter or margarine, melted
¾ c. chopped almonds or pecans
1 lg. tart apple, shredded
1 c. shredded carrot
½ c. raisins
½ c. matzo meal
½ c. sugar
3 T. lemon juice
1 tsp. cinnamon

Beat egg whites until stiff. Set aside. Combine butter, nuts, yolks and remaining ingredients. Fold in egg whites. Pour into greased 2½-quart casserole. Bake at 375° for 40 minutes.

5-6 servings

PASSOVER APPLE COFFEE CAKE

Show ■
Go ☐

¾ c. sugar
2 tsp. cinnamon
5 tart apples, peeled, cored and sliced
juice of 1 lemon
6 eggs
1¾ c. sugar
1 c. peanut oil
2 c. matzo cake meal
2 tsp. potato starch
dash salt
¼ c. sugar
2 tsp. cinnamon
¼ c. chopped walnuts

Combine ¾ cup sugar with 2 teaspoons cinnamon. Mix with sliced apples and lemon juice and set aside. Beat eggs with 1¾ cups sugar and add the oil. Sift together cake meal, potato starch and salt. Add to egg mixture, blending well. Pour half of batter into greased 9x13-inch cake pan. Spread apple mixture over batter. Top with rest of batter. Mix together remaining sugar and cinnamon with nuts and sprinkle over cake. Bake at 350° for 1 hour and 15 minutes or until cake tests done.

24 squares

CHOCOLATE SOUFFLE FOR PASSOVER

Show ■
Go ☐

7 (1 oz.) sq. semi-sweet chocolate
¼ c. strong coffee
7 eggs, separated
¾ c. sugar

Chocolate Mocha Cream:
8 (1 oz.) sq. semi-sweet chocolate
¼ c. strong coffee
1 c. plus 2 T. butter or margarine, softened
1½ c. powdered sugar
4 eggs
2 T. cocoa
chocolate shavings
chopped nuts

Melt 7 ounces chocolate and ¼ cup coffee. Cool slightly. Beat egg yolks with ½ cup sugar until fluffy and lemon colored. Add chocolate and coffee mixture. In separate bowl, beat egg whites until soft peaks form. Add ¼ cup sugar, gradually beating until stiff peaks form. Gently fold egg whites into chocolate. Spread batter into greased 10½x15½-inch jelly roll pan that has been lined with greased waxed paper. Bake at 350° for 15-20 minutes or until firm. Remove and cool for 5 minutes. Place a damp cloth over roll and set in a cool place.

For chocolate mocha cream, melt chocolate in coffee, stirring constantly; let cool. Cream butter and sugar and add to chocolate mixture, blending well. Add eggs, one at a time, and beat until smooth. Remove roll from pan onto fresh piece of waxed paper. When ready to use remove towel and sprinkle roll with cocoa. Spread half of the mocha filling over top and roll up starting at long end. Frost with remaining filling. Decorate top with shavings and nuts. Slice and serve. Refrigerate any leftover roll.

12 servings

If roll is too long, cut to fit size of serving plate.

Celebrate!

PASSOVER CHOCOLATE CHIFFON CAKE

Show ■
Go ■

⅔ c cold water
¼ c. cocoa
8 lg. eggs, separated
1½ c. sugar
½ c. oil
½ c. matzo cake meal
½ c. potato starch

Boil water and cocoa together until slightly thickened. Let cool. Beat egg whites, add ¼ cup sugar and beat until stiff. Set aside. Beat yolks and remaining 1¼ cup sugar together. Add chocolate mixture, oil, cake meal and starch. Mix well. Fold in whites. Pour into ungreased 10-inch angel food pan. Bake at 325° for 10 minutes. Increase heat to 350° and bake for 50 minutes. Invert to cool. Before removing from pan, run knife around cake to loosen the sides.

10-12 servings

PASSOVER CHOCOLATE CAKE

Show ■
Go ■

6 oz. semi-sweet chocolate
10 eggs, separated
¾ c. plus 2 T. sugar
2 c. finely chopped walnuts

Melt chocolate; cool. Beat egg yolks and sugar until thick and lemon colored. Stir in chocolate and fold in chopped nuts. Beat egg whites until stiff, but not dry; fold into chocolate mixture. Pour batter into a greased 10 inch springform pan. Bake at 350° for 1 hour or until center springs back when lightly touched. Cool completely; remove side of pan. Serve plain or with Fudge Sauce (see index) and whipped cream.

10-12 servings

Don't pass over this one!

PASSOVER ANGEL FOOD CAKE

Show ■
Go ■

10 lg. egg whites
¼ tsp. salt
1 T. lemon juice
2 T. orange juice
¾ c. sugar
¾ c. potato starch
¼ c. cake meal
¾ c. sugar

Beat egg whites until foamy. Add salt and juices. Beat until very thick. Gradually add ¾ cup sugar and beat until mixture forms peaks. Sift together potato starch, cake meal and ¾ cup sugar; fold into egg white mixture. Pour into 10-inch angel food pan. Bake at 350° for 45-50 minutes. Invert to cool. Before removing from pan, run knife around cake to loosen the sides.

10-12 servings

PASSOVER BROWNIES

Show ■
Go ■

1 c. sugar
½ c. butter, melted
¼ c. cocoa
2 eggs, separated and beaten
¼ c. milk
¼ tsp. salt
½ c. matzo cake meal
powdered sugar

Combine sugar, butter and cocoa together. Add beaten egg yolks, milk, salt and cake meal. Fold in beaten egg whites. Pour into greased 8x8-inch pan. Bake at 350° for 30 minutes. Dust with powdered sugar.

1-1½ dozen bars

Good enough to make all year long.

MATZO BALLS FOR PASSOVER

Show ■
Go ■

3 eggs, separated
½ tsp. salt
¾ c. matzo meal

Beat egg whites until stiff. In separate bowl beat egg yolks. Fold yolks into whites. Add salt to matzo meal and add to egg mixture. Refrigerate for 15 minutes. Wet hands and shape loosely into small balls. Drop into a very large pot of rapidly boiling salted water and cook for 45 minutes. Keep covered the entire time. Remove and add to hot soup.

14 matzo balls

PESACH PUDDING

Show ■
Go ■

¾ c. seedless raisins
1 lemon
4 cooking apples
4 eggs, separated
¼ tsp. salt
1 c. sugar
½ c. matzo meal
½ tsp. cinnamon

Rinse and drain raisins. Grate rind from lemon and squeeze juice. Peel and chop apples into small chunks. Add lemon rind and juice to apples. Beat egg whites with salt until stiff. Gradually beat in sugar. Beat yolks well and fold into egg whites. Fold in matzo meal, raisins, cinnamon and apples. Pour into greased 9x13-inch baking dish. Bake at 350° for 30 minutes. Serve warm or cold.

12 servings

MOM'S HAMANTASHEN

Show ■
Go ☐

Dough:
1 c. sugar
1 c. butter or margarine, softened
3 eggs
½ tsp. salt
rind of 1 orange
¼ c. orange juice
1 tsp vanilla
4 c. flour
3 tsp. baking powder

Filling:
8 oz. pitted prunes
8 oz. dried apricots
¼ c. raisins
¼ c. nuts (optional)
⅛ c. lemon juice
¼ tsp. cinnamon
1 (6 oz.) jar strawberry jam

For dough, using a mixer, cream together sugar and butter. Add eggs and mix well. Add remaining ingredients in order listed. Cover with waxed paper and refrigerate for several hours.

For filling, grind together prunes, apricots, raisins and nuts. Add lemon juice, cinnamon and jam. Mix thoroughly. To assemble, roll out ½ of dough on floured board. Cut into 1½ inch rounds with cookie cutter. Put a small amount of filling in center of each circle. Fold over and pinch together in triangular form. Place on greased cookie sheet. Sprinkle with sugar. Bake at 350° for 20-30 minutes or until browned.

4 dozen

WHOLE WHEAT HAMANTASHEN

Show ■
Go ☐

Dough:
½ c. butter or margarine
½ c. sugar
¼ c. honey
1 tsp. vanilla
1 tsp. vinegar
2 eggs
1½ c. whole wheat flour
1½ c. all-purpose flour
2 tsp. baking powder
1 tsp. cinnamon
½ tsp. baking soda

Raisin Poppy Seed Filling:
5 T. poppy seeds
¾ c. raisins
1½ T. honey
2 T. butter, melted
2 tsp. grated lemon rind

Apricot Filling:
½ c. finely chopped dried apricots
½ c. finely chopped almonds or walnuts
1½ T. honey
2 T. melted butter
¼ tsp. cinnamon or ginger

For dough, in large bowl, beat together butter, sugar, honey, vanilla, vinegar and eggs until well mixed. In small bowl, mix flours, baking powder, cinnamon and soda. Add to sugar mixture and blend well. Chill at least 3 hours or overnight.

Choose one filling; mix all ingredients together in small bowl. On a well floured board, roll dough to ⅛ inch thickness and cut into 3 inch circles. Set circles slightly apart on lightly greased baking sheets. Drop a generous teaspoon of one of the fillings onto center of each circle. Bring edges up to form a triangle and pinch seams together to seal. Re-roll scraps and repeat process until dough and filling are used. Bake at 350° for about 15 minutes or until edges are brown. Cool on wire rack. Store in airtight container. These freeze well.

2 dozen

Healthy days are here again!

PASSOVER GRANOLA

Show ☐
Go ■

3 c. matzo farfel
1 c. chopped walnuts or pecans
1 c. almonds, slivered
¼ c. butter
¼ c. brown sugar
¼ c. honey
chocolate chips (optional)
chopped dried fruit (optional)

Line a jelly roll pan with parchment paper. Toast matzo farfel and nuts in 350 degree oven for 15 minutes. In a saucepan, melt butter, brown sugar and honey. Bring to a boil and remove from heat. Pour over toasted matzo farfel. Stir to coat and put back in oven for 10-15 minutes. Stir again. Put back in oven for 5 minutes. Remove from oven and pour directly into a bowl or foil pan. As it cools, break large pieces. When cool, add chocolate chips or other dried fruit (optional).

Makes 5 cups.

CHOCOLATE FILLED HAMANTASHEN

Show ■
Go ☐

Dough:
4 eggs
1 c. sugar
1 c. corn oil
2 tsp. lemon juice
1¼ tsp. vanilla
⅓ c. orange juice
1 grated orange rind
4 c. flour
1 tsp. salt
2 tsp. baking powder

Chocolate filling:
12 oz. bag semi-sweet chocolate chips
1 T. butter
1 can sweetened condensed milk

Mix eggs, sugar, oil, lemon juice, vanilla, orange juice, rind, flour, salt and baking powder together. Chill dough overnight. Roll out cold dough and cut out 4 inch circles. Melt chocolate chips and butter in microwave for 1 minute 30 seconds. Add condensed milk stir until smooth. Line cookie sheets with parchment paper. Drop 1 tsp. of chocolate filling on each circle and pinch into triangle shape. Make an egg wash (1 egg with 1 T. water) and brush each cookie, sprinkle lightly with sugar. Bake at 350° for 11-12 minutes until golden brown.

Approximately 4 dozen

MOM'S MAMMOTH PASSOVER POPOVERS

Show ■
Go ■

1½ c. water
½ c. Crisco (solid)
1 T. plus 1 tsp. sugar
1 tsp. salt
1½ c. cake meal
7 eggs

Boil water, Crisco, sugar and salt. Remove from heat. Add cake meal and cool. Add eggs one at a time and beat with mixer. Preheat oven to 400 degrees. Grease 12 Pyrex cups and fill ¾ of the way with batter. Carefully place directly on oven racks. Bake for 45 minutes. Turn oven down to 375°. Bake an additional 15 minutes. Remove and serve.

12 servings

PASSOVER BLUEBERRY MUFFINS

Show ■
Go ■

1 c. sugar
⅓ c. oil
3 eggs
¼ tsp. vanilla
½ c. matzo cake meal
¼ c. potato starch
1½ c. frozen blueberries
cinnamon/sugar mixture to taste (optional)

Blend sugar and oil. Add eggs one at a time. Beat after each egg. Add vanilla, cake meal and potato starch gradually to mixture and beat well. Fold frozen blueberries into batter. Line muffin tin (12) with cupcake papers. Fill muffin cups ½ full. If desired top with sugar/cinnamon mix. Bake 350° for about 45 min.

12 servings

HEAVENLY HASH PASSOVER BROWNIES

Show ■
Go ■

4 eggs
2 c. sugar
1 c. butter
4 oz. unsweetened chocolate, melted
1 c. cake meal
¼ tsp. salt
6 oz. chocolate chips
2 c. mini marshmallows
chopped nuts (optional)

Mix together eggs, sugar, butter, chocolate, cake meal and salt. Fold in chocolate chips and marshmallows. Spread in a greased 9x13-inch pan. Bake 350° for 25 minutes. Take out and cover immediately with foil. Let cool and dust top with powdered sugar.

16 servings

SOUR CREAM HAMANTASHEN DOUGH

Show ■
Go ☐

1 ½ c. sugar
12 T. butter
2 eggs
¾ c. sour cream
1 tsp. baking soda
4½ c. flour
1 tsp. baking powder
½ tsp. salt
2 tsp. vanilla

Cream the butter and sugar in a large mixing bowl. Add eggs and sour cream in medium bowl. Combine baking soda, flour, baking powder and salt. Add flour mixture to the butter mixture and the vanilla. Chill dough for one hour. Roll dough out ¼ inch thick. Cut with a round cookie cutter. Add 1 tsp. of favorite filling to each circle. Form the Hamantashen. Bake at 375° for 15-20 minutes.

Approximately 4 dozen

Sweet Stuff

SPICY RAISIN BARS

Show ■
Go ■

1 c. raisins
1 c. water
½ c. oil
1 c. sugar
1 egg, slightly beaten
1¾ c. flour
1 tsp. salt
1 tsp. baking soda
1 tsp. cinnamon
1 tsp. nutmeg
½ tsp. cloves
½ c. chopped nuts

Frosting:
2 c. powdered sugar
¼ c. butter, melted
lemon juice

Combine raisins, water and oil and bring to a boil. Cool to lukewarm. Stir in sugar and egg. Sift dry ingredients together and add to raisin mixture. Fold in nuts. Pour into greased 9x13-inch pan. Bake at 350° for 25 minutes or until bars spring back when lightly touched. Cool. For frosting, in a small bowl; mix powdered sugar and butter. Add enough lemon juice to make smooth spreading consistency and frost bars.

32 bars

A real raisin for living

OATMEAL CARAMEL SQUARES

Show ■
Go ■

3 c. flour
3 c. quick oatmeal
2¼ c. brown sugar
1½ tsp. baking soda
¾ tsp. salt
2 c. butter, melted
3 c. chocolate chips
1½ c. chopped pecans
2 (12 oz.) jars caramel ice cream topping
6 T. flour

Mix 3 cups flour, oatmeal, brown sugar, soda and salt with butter. Press half the mixture into a greased 11½x16-inch jelly roll pan. Bake at 350° for 10 minutes. Sprinkle with chocolate chips and pecans. Mix caramel topping with 6 tablespoons flour and drizzle over chips. Sprinkle remaining batter on top and pat down. Put pan on a large cookie sheet. Bake at 350° for 20 minutes. Cool and cut into 1 inch squares.

80 squares

GRAHAM CRACKER GOODY BARS

Show ■
Go ■

2¼ c. graham cracker crumbs
1 (6 oz.) pkg. chocolate chips
1 (14 oz.) can sweetened condensed milk
1 tsp. vanilla
powdered sugar

Mix graham cracker crumbs, chocolate chips, milk and vanilla together by hand. Spread in a greased 8x8-inch pan. Bake at 350° for 20 minutes. Let stand until partially cooled. Cut into squares and roll in powdered sugar. Bars must be slightly warm or sugar will not stick. For a double recipe use a 9x13-inch pan.

16 bars

MIXED NUT BARS

Show ■
Go ■

1½ c. flour
½ c. butter, softened
¾ c. sugar
½ tsp. salt
1 (6 oz.) pkg. butterscotch chips
½ c. light corn syrup
2 T. butter
1 T. water
1 (12½ oz.) can mixed nuts

Mix flour, butter, sugar and salt together and press into an ungreased 9x13-inch pan. Bake at 350° for 10 minutes. In a saucepan, combine chips, syrup, butter and water. Heat until chips are melted. Pour over baked crust. Sprinkle mixed nuts over the top and bake another 10 minutes. Cut while warm.

24 bars

goody goody for everyone!

HERSHEY® BAR BARS

Show ■
Go ■

1 c. unsalted butter
¾ c. sugar
1 egg
2 tsp. vanilla
½ tsp. salt
2½ c. flour
3 (8 oz.) Hershey chocolate bars
powdered sugar

With hand mixer or food processor, cream butter and sugar. Add egg, vanilla, salt and flour; blend. Press half of dough into a greased 9x13-inch pan. Place chocolate bars on top. Pat remaining dough over bars and make ridges with a fork. Bake at 350° for 25 minutes, or until edges are brown and top remains light. Cut while warm. Remove from pan and sprinkle with powdered sugar.

24 bars

LEMON SOUR WALNUT BARS

Show ■
Go ■

Crust:
¾ c. flour
⅓ c. butter, softened

Filling:
1 c. brown sugar
½ tsp. vanilla
2 eggs
¾ c. flaked coconut, packed
⅛ tsp. baking powder
½ c. chopped walnuts

Glaze:
⅔ c. powdered sugar
1 T. grated lemon rind
2 T. lemon juice

For crust, blend flour and butter. Press into an ungreased 8x8-inch pan. Bake at 350° for 12 minutes. Combine all filling ingredients and pour into crust. Continue to bake for 25 minutes. Cool. For glaze, mix powdered sugar and lemon rind. Slowly stir in lemon juice to glaze consistency and pour over bars.

16 bars

DATE SQUARES

Show ■
Go ■

1½ c. flour
1½ c. quick oatmeal
½ c. butter or Crisco
1 tsp. baking soda
¾ c. brown sugar
¼ tsp. salt
1 (8 oz.) pkg. chopped dates
¾ c. sugar
¾ c. water
½ tsp. vanilla

Combine flour, oatmeal, butter, soda, brown sugar and salt with a fork. In a greased 8x8-inch pan, pat down half of the mixture. In medium saucepan, boil dates, sugar and water for a few minutes until dates are soft; add vanilla. Pour date mixture over dough. Sprinkle remaining dough on top and pat down. Bake at 350° for 20 minutes. Cool and cut into squares.

16 squares

CARROT BARS

Show ■
Go ■

4 eggs
2 c. sugar
1½ c. oil
2 c. flour
2 tsp. baking soda
1 tsp. salt
1 T. cinnamon
3 (4½ oz.) jars strained carrot baby food

Frosting:
¼ c. butter, melted
1 (8 oz.) pkg. cream cheese, softened
½ tsp. vanilla
3½-4 c. powdered sugar

In mixer bowl, beat eggs until thick. Gradually add sugar, oil, flour, soda, salt and cinnamon; mix well. Add carrots. Pour into greased 10½x15½-inch jelly roll pan. Bake at 350° for 30-40 minutes. Cool, do not overbake.

For frosting, mix together butter, cream cheese and vanilla. Slowly beat in powdered sugar until spreading consistency. Spread on cooled bars.

75 bars

A taste for sore eyes!

EDINER SUPER BROWNIES

Show ■
Go ■

1 c. flour
1 tsp. baking powder
1 tsp. salt
⅔ c. butter
5 (1 oz.) squares unsweetened chocolate
2 c. sugar
4 eggs, slightly beaten
2 tsp. vanilla
1½ c. chopped nuts

Frosting:
2 (1 oz.) sq. unsweetened chocolate
⅓ c. butter
1½ c. powdered sugar
¼ c. hot coffee

In a bowl, mix together flour, baking powder and salt. Set aside. In a large saucepan over low heat, melt butter and chocolate. Blend in sugar, eggs, vanilla and flour mixture until well combined. Stir in nuts. Pour into greased 9x13-inch pan. Bake at 350° for 20-25 minutes, until center has just set. Cool completely before frosting.

For frosting, melt chocolate and butter over low heat. Stir in sugar and coffee. Beat until smooth. Let cool before spreading on brownies.

24 bars

NEW YORK, NEW YORK BROWNIES

Show ■
Go ■

2 (1 oz.) squares unsweetened chocolate
1 c. butter
2 eggs
1 c. sugar
½ c. flour
½ tsp. vanilla
½ c. chopped pecans

Melt chocolate and butter together; cool. Mix eggs and sugar. Add melted chocolate mixture. Mix in flour, vanilla and pecans; pour into greased 8x8-inch pan. Bake at 350° for 25-30 minutes. Cut while warm.

16 bars

Enjoy... Enjoy... ENJOY!

FILTHY RICH BROWNIES

Show ■
Go ■

2 eggs
1 c. sugar
1 tsp. vanilla
½ c. butter
2 (1 oz.) squares unsweetened chocolate
½ c. chocolate chips
½ c. flour

Frosting:
¼ c. butter, softened
2 c. powdered sugar
¼ c. milk
⅓ c. cocoa
1 tsp. vanilla

Beat eggs until thick and lemon colored. Gradually add sugar and continue to beat. Add vanilla. In double boiler or microwave melt butter and chocolates. Let cool a few minutes. Combine chocolate and egg mixtures. Fold in flour. Pour into greased 9x9-inch pan. Bake at 350° for 20 minutes. Cool.

For frosting, place frosting ingredients in mixing bowl and blend until smooth. Spread on brownies. If food processor is used, make frosting with cold butter.

16-18 bars

FUDGIE BROWNIES

Show ■
Go ■

1 c. Crisco
4 (1 oz.) squares unsweetened chocolate
2 c. sugar
4 eggs
1 c. flour
1 tsp. salt
1 T. vanilla
1 c. miniature marshmallows
1 c. walnuts, in large pieces
1 c. chocolate chips (optional)
powdered sugar

Melt Crisco and chocolate together. Mix in sugar and let cool. With wooden spoon, stir in eggs, flour, salt and vanilla. Fold in marshmallows and nuts; add chocolate chips if desired. Place in greased 9x13-inch pan and bake at 350° for 20-25 minutes. Do not over bake. Sprinkle with powdered sugar.

36 bars

DOUBLE FEATURE BROWNIES

Show ■
Go ☐

1 (4 oz.) pkg. German's sweet chocolate
3 T. butter
1 (3 oz.) pkg. cream cheese, softened
2 T. butter, softened
1 c. sugar
3 eggs
1 T. flour
1½ tsp. vanilla
½ tsp. baking powder
¼ tsp. salt
½ c. flour
¼ tsp. almond extract
¼ tsp butter extract
½ c. nuts

Frosting:
½ c. chocolate chips
2 T. butter
¼ tsp. almond extract
3 T. milk
1 c. powdered sugar, sifted
chocolate shot (optional)

Melt chocolate and 3 tablespoons butter over low heat. Let cool. Mix cream cheese with 2 tablespoons butter. Slowly add ¼ cup sugar and blend thoroughly. Add 1 egg, 1 tablespoon flour and ¼ teaspoon vanilla. Set aside. In bowl, beat remaining eggs and slowly add remaining sugar. Mix well. Add baking powder, salt and ½ cup flour. Add the chocolate mixture, remaining vanilla, almond and butter extracts. Stir in nuts.

Grease and flour an 8x8-inch pan and pour in ½ of mixture. Cover with cream cheese batter and spoon on remaining chocolate mixture. Marble with knife. Bake at 350° for 35-40 minutes.

For frosting; in saucepan over low heat, combine chocolate chips, butter, almond extract and milk. Stir until chocolate is melted. Remove from heat. Stir in powdered sugar and beat until glossy and easy to spread. Frost brownies and sprinkle with chocolate shot. Recipe may be doubled and baked in 9x13-inch pan.

16 bars

Be careful, it's easy to O.D. on these!

YUM YUM COOKIES

Show ■
Go ■

1 c. butter, softened
1 c. brown sugar
1 c. sugar
2 eggs
2 tsp. vanilla
½ c. raisins or chopped dates
½ c. chopped walnuts
½ c. flaked coconut
2 c. quick oatmeal
2 c. flour
1 tsp. salt
1 tsp. baking soda

Cream butter and sugars. Add eggs, vanilla, dates, walnuts and coconut. Stir in remaining ingredients. Drop by teaspoonfuls onto greased cookie sheet. Flatten with glass dipped in sugar. Bake at 350° for 10 minutes.

8 dozen

CHOCOLATE DIPPED TREATS

Show ■
Go □

1 c. butter, softened
¾ c. powdered sugar
1 tsp. vanilla
2 c. flour

Frosting:
2 (1 oz.) squares unsweetened chocolate
2 c. powdered sugar
drops of milk

Cream butter, sugar and vanilla. Add flour and blend well. Shape dough into crescent shapes or round balls. Bake on ungreased cookie sheet at 350° for 15 minutes. Cool on rack.

For frosting, melt chocolate in double boiler. Mix in powdered sugar. Add a few drops of milk until frosting is desired consistency for dipping. Dip end or top of each cookie into chocolate and let stand on rack to cool.

To vary, sprinkle chopped nuts, chocolate or colored sprinkles on freshly dipped cookies.

4-5 dozen

OATMEAL CHOCOLATE CHIP COOKIES

Show ☐
Go ■

½ c. vegetable shortening
½ c. butter or margarine, softened
¾ c. brown sugar
¾ c. sugar
2 eggs, slightly beaten
1½ tsp. vanilla
1 T. hot water
2 c. flour
1½ tsp. baking soda
½ tsp. salt
1 c. chocolate chips
1½ c. quick oatmeal
1 c. chopped walnuts

Cream shortening, butter and sugars. Add eggs. Stir in vanilla and water. Sift together flour, baking soda and salt, and add to creamed mixture. Stir in chocolate chips, oatmeal and nuts. Drop by teaspoonfuls onto ungreased cookie sheets. Bake at 350° for 8-10 minutes or until light brown.

4-5 dozen

OATMEAL CRISPS

Show ■
Go ■

3 c. packed brown sugar
6 c. quick oatmeal
3 c. butter, softened
1 T. baking soda
3 c. flour

Place all ingredients in a large bowl. Knead by hand into a well-packed firm dough. Refrigerate for 30 minutes. Shape into small balls. Place on ungreased cookie sheet. Flatten with glass dipped in sugar. Bake at 350° for 10-12 minutes.

13 dozen

May be half dipped in melted chocolate for fancy occasion.

So nice to come home to!

MY MOM'S CINNAMON COOKIES

Show ■
Go ■

3 eggs
¾ c. brown sugar
1 c. oil
1 tsp. baking powder
¼ tsp. baking soda
2½ c. flour
¼ tsp. salt
1 tsp. vanilla
½ c. sugar
1 tsp. cinnamon

Beat eggs. Add sugar and oil; continue beating. Mix in baking powder, soda, flour, salt and vanilla. Dough will be stiff. Oil hands and shape dough into small balls. Roll in mixture of sugar and cinnamon. Place on greased cookie sheet. Bake at 350° for 10 minutes. These freeze well.

5 dozen

COOKIE BRITTLE

Show ■
Go ■

1 c. butter or margarine
1½ tsp. vanilla
1 tsp. salt
1 c. sugar
2 c. flour
1 (6 oz.) pkg. chocolate chips
½ c. finely chopped nuts
powdered sugar

In mixer or food processor, cream butter, vanilla, salt and sugar. Add flour. Mix in chocolate chips by hand. Pat into ungreased 10½x15½-inch jelly roll pan. Sprinkle nuts on top. Bake at 375° for 20-25 minutes or until lightly browned. Cool. Break into irregular pieces and drain on absorbent paper. Dust with powdered sugar.

20-30 pieces

SESAME CRESCENTS

Show ■
Go ☐

6 T. sugar
6 T. oil
2 eggs, beaten
6 T. flour
2½ c. sesame seeds

Mix together all ingredients and refrigerate for 3 hours. Divide dough in half and place on waxed paper. Using wet hands, roll dough into strips ½ inch in diameter. Cut strips into 1½ inch pieces. Shape into crescents and place on foil-lined cookie sheets. Bake at 350° for 15-20 minutes or until brown.

5-6 dozen

POPPY SEED COOKIES

Show ☐
Go ■

½ c. butter, softened
½ c. sugar
¼ tsp. vanilla
1 egg
2 c. flour
½ tsp. baking powder
¼ c. poppy seeds

Cream butter, sugar and vanilla. Add egg, flour, baking powder and poppy seeds. Blend well. Divide dough into 2 equal parts and roll into logs 1½ inches in diameter. Wrap each log in waxed paper and place in freezer. When firm, slice thinly and place on greased or teflon cookie sheets. Bake at 375° for 10-15 minutes. Watch carefully.

5½ dozen

APPLE STRUDEL

Show ■
Go ☐

5-6 firm apples, peeled and thinly sliced
2 tsp. cinnamon
¼ c. sugar
1 c. brown sugar
½ c. golden raisins
4 oz. chopped pecans
1 pkg. fillo strudel leaves
1 c. butter, melted
graham cracker crumbs, for sprinkling
1 (16 oz.) jar cherry preserves

Place apples in large bowl. Add cinnamon, sugars, raisins and nuts. Mix well. For 1 strudel roll, unfold fillo leaves and place 1 leaf on a towel. Cover remaining leaves with moist towel. Brush leaf with butter and sprinkle with cracker crumbs. Place a second leaf on top and repeat butter and crumbs process until there are 6 fillo sheets.

With slotted spoon, take ⅓ of apple mixture and place on long end of leaf. Put ⅓ of cherry preserves along top of apple mixture. Roll up like jelly roll; brush with butter and place on buttered jelly roll pan. Repeat for two more rolls. Make slits 2 inches apart on top. Bake at 375° for 35 minutes. Slice and serve warm with ice cream.

Freezes well in foil. To serve, thaw in refrigerator overnight. Place on jelly roll pan and open foil. Heat at 325° about 20 minutes.

3 rolls, 6-8 servings per roll

SPONGE CAKE WITH LEMON FILLING

Show ■
Go ☐

6 eggs, separated
1 c. sugar
¼ c. cold water
1 tsp. lemon extract
1 tsp. grated lemon rind
1 c. sifted cake flour
½ tsp. cream of tartar
½ tsp. salt

Filling and Frosting:
1 c. sugar
3 T. cornstarch
½ tsp. salt
1 c. water
2 T. grated lemon rind
½ c. lemon juice
2 T. butter
4 egg yolks
coconut

Beat 6 egg yolks until thick, at least 5 minutes. Gradually beat in sugar. Combine water, lemon extract and rind; beat alternately with flour into yolks. In large bowl, beat 6 egg whites, cream of tartar and salt until stiff. Gently fold yolk mixture into whites and pour into ungreased 10-inch tube pan. Bake at 325° for 60-65 minutes. When cake springs back when touched lightly on top, invert until completely cool.

For filling, mix sugar, cornstarch, salt, water, lemon rind, juice and butter in saucepan. Bring to rolling boil and boil 1 minute, stirring constantly. Remove from heat and beat in egg yolks. Return to heat and cook 1 minute more, stirring constantly. Chill. Cut cake into 2 layers and spread with filling. Frost sides and top. Sprinkle with coconut.

10-12 servings

GATEAU CHOCOLAT

Show ■
Go ☐

15 oz. Tobler bittersweet chocolate bars
14 T. butter
10 eggs, separated
1½ c. sugar
2 T. Grand Marnier liqueur
2 tsp. vanilla
powdered sugar
whipped cream

Melt chocolate and butter together. Add egg yolks, sugar, liqueur and vanilla. Beat egg whites until stiff and gently fold into mixture. Pour into a well greased 10-inch springform pan. Bake at 275° for 2¼ hours. Cake will rise and fall during baking and crumble when crust is cut. Sprinkle with powdered sugar and serve warm with dab of whipped cream.

16 servings

FRANGELICO RUM CAKE

Show ■
Go ☐

1 c. chopped nuts
2 T. sugar
1 (3¾ oz.) pkg. instant vanilla pudding
4 eggs
½ c. water
½ c. oil
¼ c. rum
¼ c. Frangelico or Amaretto liqueur
1 (18 oz.) pkg. yellow cake mix

Syrup:
½ c. butter
¼ c. water
1 c. sugar
¼ c. rum
¼ c. Frangelico or Amaretto liqueur

Mix nuts and 2 tablespoons sugar. Sprinkle in bottom of well-greased and floured bundt pan. Blend in mixer for 5 minutes or food processor for 1 minute; the pudding, eggs, water, oil, rum and liqueur. Add cake mix and blend well in mixer or until it is completely blended in processor. Pour into bundt pan. Bake at 325° for 1 hour. Leave in pan. While warm, poke lots of holes with a fork in cake.

For syrup, combine butter, water and sugar in medium saucepan. Boil 5 minutes, stirring constantly. Add rum and Frangelico. Pour hot syrup over cake. Cool cake completely in pan before removing.

10-12 servings

RHUBARB CAKE

Show ■
Go ■

1½ c. brown sugar
½ c. butter or margarine, softened
1 egg
2 c. flour
½ tsp. salt
1 tsp. baking soda
1 c. buttermilk
3 c. diced rhubarb
1 c. chopped nuts
½ c. sugar
2 tsp. cinnamon

In mixing bowl, cream sugar and butter. Add egg. Combine flour, salt and soda; add alternately with buttermilk to creamed mixture. Stir in rhubarb and nuts. Pour into 9x13 inch pan. Combine sugar and cinnamon and sprinkle on top. Bake at 350° for 40 minutes. May be served warm or cold. Freezes well.

24 servings

CHOCOLATE TOFFEE CAKE

Show ■
Go ■

1 (10 inch) angel food cake

Toffee:
1 c. butter
1 c. sugar
1 c. whole blanched almonds

Frosting:
½ c. butter
2 c. powdered sugar
4 eggs
1 tsp. vanilla
8 oz. bittersweet chocolate, melted

Cut cake into 3 layers. For toffee, slowly melt 1 cup butter and 1 cup sugar in saucepan. Increase heat; add almonds and stir until mixed. Continue to cook and stir about 10 minutes or until coffee colored. Watch carefully. Pour into ungreased 8x10-inch pan; cool. Chop into bite-size pieces when hard.

For frosting, cream butter and powdered sugar; mix in eggs one at a time. Stir in vanilla and melted chocolate; beat until mixed. Add more powdered sugar if frosting is too thin.

Spread frosting on bottom layer of cake and sprinkle generously with toffee pieces. Place second cake layer on top and repeat process. Add third layer and frost entire cake top and sides. Sprinkle remaining toffee over cake.

12-14 servings

May substitute crushed Heath or Almond Roca bars for toffee as a time saver.

TEXAS CHOCOLATE SHEET CAKE

Show ■
Go ■

2 c. sugar
2 c. flour
½ tsp. salt
1 c. butter
1 c. water
3 T. unsweetened cocoa
½ c. dairy sour cream
2 eggs
1 tsp. baking soda
dash of cinnamon

Frosting:
¼ c. butter or shortening
⅓ c. unsweetened cocoa
2 c. powdered sugar
¼ c. milk
1 tsp. vanilla

In a large bowl, combine sugar, flour and salt; set aside. In a small saucepan, bring butter, water and cocoa to a boil. Remove from heat. Add to dry ingredients and mix well. Add sour cream, eggs, soda and cinnamon and blend well. Pour into greased and lightly floured 10½x15½-inch jelly roll pan. Bake at 375° for 20-25 minutes. Do not over bake. For frosting, melt butter and cocoa together. Add remaining ingredients and blend until smooth. Spread on cake.

40 pieces

Looks like a brownie, tastes like a cake!

CHEESECAKE SUPREME

Show ■
Go ■

Crust:
3 c. graham cracker crumbs
½ c. sugar
½ c. butter, melted

Filling:
5 (8 oz.) pkg. cream cheese
1 (3 oz.) pkg. cream cheese
1½ c. sugar
5 eggs
2 c. sour cream
1½ tsp. vanilla
juice of one lemon

For crust, mix together graham cracker crumbs, ½ cup sugar and butter. Press into bottom of 10½-inch springform pan. For filling, in a large bowl at medium speed, beat together cream cheese, 1½ cups sugar and eggs for 15 minutes. Add sour cream, vanilla and lemon juice. Beat an additional 15 minutes. Pour into prepared pan. Bake at 350° for 55 minutes. Turn off oven and let cheesecake remain in oven for 2 hours. Remove and cool. Refrigerate.

12 servings

CHOCOLATE SWIRL CHEESECAKE

Show ■
Go ■

Crust:
4½ oz. chocolate cookie wafers
2 T. sugar
1 tsp. cinnamon
¼ c. unsalted butter, melted

Filling:
1 (6 oz.) pkg. chocolate chips
3 (8 oz.) pkgs. cream cheese, softened
4 lg. eggs
1 c. sugar
1 tsp. vanilla

In food processor or blender, crumble the wafers. Add sugar, cinnamon and butter; mix well. Press mixture into a greased 8-inch springform pan and set aside.

For filling, melt chocolate. In large mixing bowl or food processor, cream the cheese. Add eggs and blend. Slowly add sugar, then vanilla and blend thoroughly. Pour all but 3 tablespoons batter into crust. Mix melted chocolate with remaining batter to form a stiff paste. Drop dollops of chocolate mixture on top of cheesecake batter. Swirl by running a knife through and around in zigzag motion.

With aluminum foil, make a collar about 3 inches high. Fit around edge of pan, pinching to attach to edge and bend collar in a little to protect cheesecake. Bake at 375° for 1¼-1½ hours. Cheesecake is done when it has risen, is firm in center and has cracked around edge. Remove from oven, let cool and refrigerate overnight in springform pan. Before serving, remove springform and drizzle top with melted chocolate, if desired.

10-12 servings

Oohs and ahs!

PRALINE CHEESECAKE

Show ■
Go ■

Crust:
1 c. graham cracker crumbs
3 T. sugar
3 T. butter, melted

Filling:
3 (8 oz.) pkgs. cream cheese, softened
1½ c. dark brown sugar
2 T. flour
3 eggs
1½ tsp. vanilla
½ c. finely chopped pecans
maple syrup
pecans, coarsely broken

Mix cracker crumbs with sugar and butter. Blend well and press into 9 inch springform pan. Bake at 350 degrees for 10 minutes. For filling, combine cream cheese, sugar and flour until well blended. Beat in eggs, one at a time. Add vanilla and nuts. Pour over crust and bake at 350° for 50-55 minutes. Cake will pull away from sides and top will crack. May be frozen at this point. Brush top with lots of syrup, letting it fill cracks. Cover with broken pecans.

12-14 servings

CHOCOLATE CHEESECAKE

Show ■
Go ☐

Crust:
1 (9 oz.) pkg. chocolate cookie wafers, crushed
¼ c. butter, melted

Filling:
4 (8 oz.) pkgs. cream cheese, softened
1 c. sugar
4 eggs
2 (1 oz.) squares semi-sweet chocolate
1 T. butter
½ pt. whipping cream
2 T. powdered sugar
½ tsp. vanilla
chocolate curls

For crust, combine wafers and melted butter and press onto side and bottom of a greased 10-inch springform pan. Chill while preparing filling.

For filling, blend 8 ounces cream cheese with ¼ cup sugar and 1 egg in food processor or mixer. Repeat this process three times, beating well after each addition. Melt chocolate and butter and add to creamed mixture; pour over cooled crust. Bake at 350° for 25-30 minutes. Turn off heat, leave oven door half open for 30 minutes. Remove cheesecake from oven and cool. Whip cream with powdered sugar and vanilla. Spread over cream cheese layer and garnish with chocolate curls.

12-14 servings

COCONUT CUSTARD PIE

Show ■
Go ■

1 c. freshly grated coconut or 1 (3½ oz.)
    can flaked coconut
3 eggs
¼ c. butter, softened
½ c. flour
½ tsp. baking powder
1 c. sugar
¼ tsp. salt
1 tsp. vanilla
1 tsp. grated lime rind
2 c. milk
3 T. coconut rum (or 1 T. cream of
    coconut with 2 T. white rum)

Place all ingredients in blender and process until combined. Pour mixture into a 10 inch greased pie plate and bake at 350° for 1 hour. Sprinkle coconut on top if desired. Chill and serve.

12 servings

CHOCOLATE CHIP PECAN PIE

Show ■
Go ■

1 c. sugar
4 eggs
1 c. light corn syrup
1 tsp. vanilla
½ c. butter
1 c. chopped pecans
1 (6 oz.) pkg. chocolate chips
1 unbaked 10 inch pie shell, regular or
    graham cracker

Combine sugar, eggs, syrup, vanilla and mix well. Melt butter, cool and add to mixture. Fold in pecans and chocolate chips, stirring until well mixed. Pour into pie shell. Bake at 350° for 50 minutes or until set.

6-8 servings

BUSTER BAR DESSERT

Show ■
Go ■

1 lb. Oreo cookies
½ c. butter or margarine, melted
½ gal. vanilla ice cream, softened
1½ c. Spanish peanuts
2 c. powdered sugar
⅔ c. chocolate chips
1½ c. evaporated milk
½ c. butter
1 tsp. vanilla

Crush cookies in food processor or with rolling pin. Mix cookies with ½ cup butter and pat in 9x13-inch pan. Spread ice cream over cookies. Top with peanuts. Freeze. Combine powdered sugar, chocolate chips, milk and ½ cup butter in a saucepan. Slowly bring to a boil and simmer 8 minutes, stirring constantly. Remove from heat and add vanilla. Cool and spread over ice cream and nuts. Freeze until ready to serve.

12 servings

Rx for a rainy day

COOKIE SUNDAE PIE

Show ■
Go ☐

Shell:
3 egg whites
pinch of salt
¾ c. sugar
12 Oreo cookies, crushed
½ c. chopped pecans
¼ tsp. vanilla
pinch of cream of tartar

Filling:
½ gal. ice cream, favorite flavor
Hot Fudge Sauce (see index)

To make shell, beat egg whites and salt until soft peaks form. Gradually add sugar and continue beating until peaks become stiff. Fold cookies, pecans, vanilla and cream of tartar. Pour into a greased 8-inch pie plate. Bake at 325° for 30-35 minutes. Cool. Smash down crust and place ice cream on top. Freeze. Serve with Hot Fudge Sauce.

6 servings

COFFEE FUDGE PIE

Show ■
Go ■

½ c. slivered almonds
1 T. butter
3 egg whites
1 c. sugar
1 tsp. vanilla
¾ c. chopped walnuts or pecans
½ c. finely-crushed saltines
1 tsp. baking powder
1 qt. coffee ice cream, softened
12 oz. fudge sauce

Sauté almonds in butter until golden. Let cool. Beat egg whites until stiff. Add sugar gradually and add vanilla. Mix nuts, saltines and baking powder; fold into egg whites. Spread on well greased 9 inch pie plate, building up sides. Bake at 300° for 40 minutes until dry on the outside. Cool. Fill with one half of ice cream and spread with fudge sauce. Add remaining ice cream, rest of fudge sauce and sprinkle with almonds. Freeze.

8-10 servings

BUTTER BRICKLE PIE

Show ■
Go ■

2 c. gingersnap crumbs
6 T. butter, melted
½ gal. vanilla ice cream, softened
1 (6 oz.) pkg. Bits 'O Brickle

Sauce:
½ c. brown sugar
½ c. whipping cream
¼ c. butter
½ c. toasted almonds
1 tsp. vanilla

Combine gingersnap crumbs and butter. Press into greased 9 inch pie plate. Freeze for 30 minutes. Mix ice cream and brickle together. Spread on pie crust. Cover tightly and freeze until ready to use. For sauce, combine sugar, cream and butter in saucepan. Bring to boil, stirring constantly. Remove from heat. Stir in almonds and vanilla. Pass hot sauce with pie.

6-8 servings

May use butter brickle ice cream to make it more "on the go".

BLUEBERRY SOUR CREAM TORTE

Show ■
Go ☐

Crust:
¾ c. butter, softened
¼ c. sugar
2 egg yolks
2 c. flour
1 tsp. baking powder
½ tsp. salt

Filling:
4 c. fresh blueberries
¾ c. sugar
¼ c. quick cooking tapioca
½ tsp. grated lemon rind
½ tsp. cinnamon
⅛ tsp. nutmeg

Topping:
2 egg yolks, slightly beaten
2 c. dairy sour cream
½ c. sugar
1 tsp. vanilla

For crust, cream butter and sugar. Add egg yolks and beat until fluffy. Combine flour, baking powder and salt and blend into creamed mixture. Press ⅔ of mixture in a 9 inch springform pan. Bake at 400° for 10 minutes. Cool. Reduce oven temperature to 350°. Press remaining crust mixture 1½ inches up side of pan.

For filling, combine berries, sugar, tapioca, lemon rind and spices in saucepan. Let stand 15 minutes. Cook and stir until bubbly and pour into crust.

For topping, blend egg yolks, sour cream, sugar and vanilla. Spoon over fruit filling and bake 350° for 45 minutes. Let cool and refrigerate until well chilled.

12 servings

Cause for celebration!

FROZEN LEMON TORTE

Show ■
Go ☐

5 eggs, separated
juice of 4 lemons
rind of 1 lemon
2 c. sugar
1 pt. whipping cream
1½ tsp. vanilla
2 (3 oz.) pkgs. ladyfingers
dash of sugar

Beat all 5 egg yolks with 2 egg whites. Cook the egg mixture, lemon juice rind and sugar in a double boiler until very thick. Cool thoroughly. Whip the cream with vanilla until stiff. Fold into lemon mixture. Line bottom and sides of a 9-inch springform pan with ladyfingers. Pour lemon mixture in pan and freeze overnight. Before serving, beat 3 egg whites and a dash of sugar until stiff. Pile on frozen torte and place under broiler until lightly browned. Watch carefully. Serve immediately or refreeze.

10-12 servings

LINZERTORTE

Show ■
Go ☐

1½ c. butter
1 c. powdered sugar
1 egg
1½ c. ground filbert nuts
pinch of salt
½ tsp. cinnamon
2¾ c. flour
2 c. raspberry jam
2 tsp. lemon juice
powdered sugar

Cream butter and sugar until light and fluffy. Add egg. Mix together nuts, salt and cinnamon. Stir flour and nut mixture alternately into creamed mixture. Chill dough. Press dough in a 9 inch springform pan, making a 1 inch rim up the side. Reserve a little dough for lattice strips on top. Mix 1½ cups jam and juice and spread over dough. Cut reserved strips of dough and form lattice over jam. Bake at 375° for 40 minutes. When cool, fill squares formed by lattice with extra jam. Sprinkle with powdered sugar.

12-14 servings

CINNAMON TORTE

Show ■
Go ☐

1½ c. butter
2 c. sugar
2 eggs
2¾ c. flour
2 T. cinnamon butter
½ c. sugar
1 tsp. cinnamon

Filling:
1½ pt. whipping cream
1 (1 oz.) square semi-sweet chocolate, grated

Topping:
½ pt. whipping cream
2 T. cocoa
2 T. powdered sugar
1 (1 oz.) sq. semi-sweet chocolate, grated

Garnish:
5 maraschino cherries, drained and dried
sliced almonds
2 T. shaved chocolate

Cream 1½ cups butter and 2 cups sugar. Add eggs. Mix flour and 2 tablespoons cinnamon together and add to creamed mixture. Cut out 16 (9 inch diameter) waxed paper circles. Grease well with butter. Using floured hands, press ⅓ cup of dough to cover each waxed paper circle. Place 2 circles on a greased cookie sheet and bake at 325° for 7 minutes.

Remove from oven; let set 30 seconds, invert onto cooling rack and peel off waxed paper. Mix ½ c. sugar and 1 teaspoon cinnamon and sprinkle a little on waxed paper side of cookie. Cool on rack. Repeat process with remaining circles. Cookies may be made ahead and frozen with waxed paper between each cookie.

For filling, whip cream. Place one cookie on a flat serving dish. Spread with thin layer of whipped cream (about 3 tablespoons per layer). Sprinkle with small amount of grated chocolate. Continue layering with remaining cookies, whipped cream and chocolate. Top with a plain cookie.

For topping, whip cream. Fold in cocoa, powdered sugar and grated chocolate. Spread on top of plain cookie. Do not frost sides. Refrigerate overnight. Before serving, garnish with cherries, almonds and shaved chocolate.

16-18 servings

RHUBARB TORTE

Show ■
Go ☐

Crust:
1 c. Crisco
2 c. flour
2 T. sugar

Filling:
6 egg yolks
2 c. sugar
1 c. half and half cream
¼ c. flour
5 c. diced rhubarb
2 tsp. grated orange rind

Meringue:
6 egg whites
6 T. sugar
¼ tsp. cream of tartar
1 tsp. vanilla
pinch of salt

For crust, mix Crisco, flour and sugar by hand or in food processor. Mixture should be crumbly like a pie crust. Pat into ungreased 9x13 inch pan. Bake at 350° for 10 minutes. For filling, mix together egg yolks, sugar, cream, flour, rhubarb and orange rind. Pour over crust and bake at 350° for 45-50 minutes or until set.

For meringue, beat egg whites until they form a soft peak. Add sugar, cream of tartar, vanilla and salt; spread over filling. Bake at 400° for 2-3 minutes until meringue is golden brown. Cool.

12-14 servings

CHOCOLATE MINT TORTE

Show ■
Go ■

Crust:
1 c. chocolate wafer crumbs
2 T. butter, melted

Filling:
½ c. butter, softened
¾ c. sugar
3 (1 oz.) squares unsweetened chocolate, melted
1 tsp. vanilla
¾ tsp. peppermint extract
3 eggs
½ c. whipping cream, whipped
shaved chocolate

Combine wafer crumbs and butter. Pat mixture on bottom only of a 9-inch springform pan. Bake at 350° for 7 minutes. Cool. For filling, beat butter until creamy. Gradually add sugar and continue beating until light and fluffy. Mix in chocolate, vanilla and peppermint. Add eggs, one at a time, beating 3 minutes after each addition. Fold in whipped cream. Spoon mixture on crust and sprinkle with shaved chocolate. Freezes well.

10-12 servings

CARAMEL NUT TORTE

Show ■
Go ☐

Crust:
3⅓ c. flour
¼ c. sugar
pinch of salt
1 c. plus 2 T. butter, cut in pieces
2 egg yolks, beaten with 6 T. cold water

Filling:
1½ c. sugar
pinch of cream of tartar
½ c. water
3½ c. chopped pecans or walnuts
½ c. butter
1 c. whipping cream
⅓ c. honey

Icing:
6 oz. semi-sweet chocolate
¼ c. butter
pinch of salt
¾ T. oil

16 pecan or walnut halves

Rich and gooey!

For crust combine flour, sugar and salt in mixer bowl. Beat in butter and egg yolks. Shape into a ball and wrap in waxed paper. Refrigerate 30 minutes only. Roll ⅔ of dough into a 13 inch floured circle. Drape over rolling pin and fit into an ungreased 11 inch flan pan. Leave ¼ inch overhang.

For filling, in a large heavy saucepan, combine sugar, cream of tartar and water. Bring to a boil. Cover and continue boiling over medium heat 1-2 minutes. Uncover and boil until mixture is a light caramel color. This will take about 8 minutes. Remove from heat. Add nuts, butter, and whipping cream. Cook over medium heat 5 minutes, reduce to simmer and cook 15 minutes. Stir in honey. Cool slightly. Pour into prepared flan pan.

Roll out remaining dough into an 11 inch circle. Drape over rolling pin and place circle on top of filling. Brush the over-hanging bottom dough with water and press over top dough. Cut a 1 inch slit in center of dough and bake at 425° for 20 minutes or until golden brown. Cool at least 4 hours and remove from pan.

For icing, melt chocolate. Add butter, salt and oil; mix well. Spread over top and sides of torte. Decorate with pecan or walnut halves.

16 servings

May be frozen before frosting – but bring to room temperature before spreading icing.

APRICOT CHOCOLATE TORTE

Show ■
Go ☐

Crust:
3 (1 oz.) sq. unsweetened chocolate
2 c. whole walnuts
1½ c. flour
¾ c. light brown sugar, firmly packed
½ tsp. salt
½ c. cold butter, cut into pieces
2 tsp. cold water
2 tsp. vanilla

Filling:
1 (11 oz.) pkg. dried apricots,
   finely chopped
1½ c. sugar
¾ c. water
3 T. flour
juice of ½ lemon
chocolate shavings

To make crust, place chocolate and nuts in food processor and chop coarsely. Add flour, sugar and salt; blend. (Bits of chocolate and nuts should be visible.) Add butter and process to blend. Add water and vanilla and mix until crumbly. Pat ⅔ of dough onto bottom and 1 inch up the sides in an 8 or 9-inch ungreased springform pan.

Prepare filling in a heavy saucepan by combining all ingredients except chocolate shavings. Bring to boil slowly over low heat. Reduce heat and simmer about 25 minutes, stirring frequently and mashing any large pieces of apricot until mixture resembles thick jam. Remove from heat and cool. Place filling in crust and crumble additional dough over top to cover. Bake at 350° for 40 minutes and cool.

To serve; remove springform and decorate top with chocolate shavings.

10-12 servings

TIA MARIA TORTE

Show ■
Go ■

2 lbs. crisp chocolate chip cookies
1 c. milk
6 oz. Tia Maria liqueur
1 pt. whipping cream
3 T. powdered sugar
1 tsp. vanilla
shaved chocolate
sliced almonds

Dip cookies in milk and then in liqueur. Arrange some cookies on bottom and sides of 8 inch springform pan. Whip cream with sugar and vanilla. Alternate whipped cream with layer of dipped cookies, ending with whipped cream. Top with chocolate and almonds. Refrigerate.

12-15 servings

STRAWBERRY PIZZA

Show ■
Go ☐

Crust:
1 c. flour
¼ c. powdered sugar
½ c. frozen unsalted butter

Filling:
1 (8 oz.) pkg. cream cheese, softened
½ c. sugar
1 tsp. vanilla
½ tsp almond extract
1 qt. fresh strawberries, washed, hulled
   and dried

Glaze:
1 (6 oz.) jar red currant jelly
1½ T. lemon juice
whipped cream

For crust, cut flour, powdered sugar and butter together. Pat evenly over a 12 or 13-inch greased pizza pan. Press firmly and bake at 325° for 15-20 minutes until lightly browned. Cool.

For filling, combine cream cheese, sugar, vanilla and almond extract, and spread over cooled crust. On filling, arrange strawberries in circles starting at outside edge and ending with a large strawberry in the center.

Make glaze by heating jelly over low heat until melted. Add lemon juice. Drizzle glaze over fruit. Top with whipped cream.

10 servings

May use fresh fruits such as kiwi, grapes, raspberries, pineapple.

CHOCOLATE "HIPPO"

Show ■
Go ■

1 pt. whipping cream
1 (16 oz.) can Hershey's chocolate syrup
1-3 T. Grand Marnier, Creme de Cacao or
   Kirsch liqueur
chocolate shavings

Whip cream until it is very stiff. Fold in chocolate syrup and liqueur thoroughly. Place in miniature souffle cups and freeze. Serve frozen. Sprinkle chocolate shavings on top of each souffle.

14 servings

ECLAIR SQUARES

Show ■
Go ■

12 oz. (approximately 21) graham crackers

Filling:
2 (3¾ oz.) pkgs. French vanilla instant
   pudding
3 c. milk
1 (8 oz.) carton Cool Whip, thawed

Frosting:
2 (1 oz.) sq. unsweetened chocolate
2 T. light corn syrup
3 T. butter or margarine
1½ c. powdered sugar
3 T. milk
½ tsp. vanilla

Prepare one to two days before serving. Lightly butter a 9x13-inch pan. Spread one layer of graham crackers on bottom of pan. Beat pudding and milk in a large bowl. Blend in Cool Whip. Cover with half of pudding mixture. Repeat layer process again, ending with graham crackers.

For frosting, melt chocolate and add remaining ingredients. Blend well and spread on top of graham crackers. Refrigerate for one to two days before serving.

16 pieces

BANANAS FOSTER BLUE HORSE

Show ■
Go ■

1 c. butter
1 c. brown sugar
1 oz. Creme de Banana liqueur
4 med. bananas
1 oz. white rum
4 scoops vanilla ice cream

In a crepe pan or 10-inch skillet, melt butter and brown sugar. Add Creme de Banana and blend thoroughly. Cut peeled bananas in half lengthwise and once crosswise, and place flat side down into mixture. Sauté on both sides until tender. Now for show, heat rum in small pan, pour over bananas and light with a match. Spoon banana mixture over ice cream in serving dishes.

4 servings

PEARL SUGAR GINGER COOKIES

Show ■
Go ■

2 c. flour
2 tsp. baking soda
½ tsp. salt
½ tsp. cinnamon
¼ tsp. cloves
¼ tsp. ginger
¾ c. butter, softened
1 c. sugar
1 egg, unbeaten
¼ c. molasses
½ c. Swedish Pearl sugar

Sift together first six ingredients, set aside. Cream butter and sugar together. Add egg and molasses, beat well. Blend in dry ingredients. Roll into 1-1½-inch balls. Dip into Pearl sugar. Bake, sugar side up, on ungreased cookie sheet for 8-10 minutes at 350°. Cookies will be crisp.

4 dozen

BEST EVER CHOCOLATE CHIP BUNDT CAKE

Show ■
Go ☐

1 bar (4 oz.) German's sweet chocolate-grated
1 pkg. plain yellow cake mix
1 pkg. (3.4 oz) instant vanilla pudding
1 c. whole milk
1 c. vegetable oil
4 lg. eggs
1 c. semi-sweet mini chocolate chips
powdered sugar

Place oven rack in center of oven. Preheat to 350 degrees. Lightly mist bundt pan or three 8-inch loaf pans with non-stick spray. Grate German's chocolate bar and set aside. Place cake mix, pudding, milk, oil and eggs in mixing bowl. Blend at low speed for 3 minutes. Reserve ¼ c. of grated chocolate and fold remaining into batter. Mix at medium speed for 2-3 minutes. Fold in chocolate chips. Pour batter into pan and bake for 50 minutes. Remove from pan and while still warm, sift together powdered sugar and remaining ¼ c. of chocolate and sprinkle on top.

16 servings

BAVARIAN APPLE CHEESE TART

Show ■
Go ■

Crust:
1 c. butter, softened
⅔ c. sugar
½ tsp. vanilla
2 c. flour

Filling:
16 oz. cream cheese, softened
½ c. sugar
2 eggs
½ tsp. vanilla
⅓ c. sugar
½ tsp. cinnamon

5 apples, pared and sliced
almonds, sliced (optional)

Crust: Grease a 12-inch fluted tart pan. Cream butter, sugar and vanilla in large mixing bowl. Blend in flour. Press dough into prepared pan to make a fairly thin crust. Spread to edges. Filling: Combine cream cheese and ½ c. sugar in a bowl. Add eggs and vanilla, mix well. Pour over crust. Combine ⅓ c. sugar, cinnamon and apples. Arrange apples decoratively over top of filling. Sprinkle with almonds. DO NOT preheat oven. Bake at 450° for 10 min. Reduce heat to 400° and bake for 25 minutes. Serve warm or cold.

8-10 servings

2007 SHOLOM ALLIANCE AWARD WINNING PUMPKIN BUNDT CAKE

Show ■
Go ■

Batter:
1 pkg. yellow cake mix
2 eggs
1 (15 oz.) can pumpkin
½ tsp. ginger
1 tsp. cinnamon
¼ tsp. ground cloves

Icing:
¾ c. powdered sugar, sifted
1½ T. milk
1 tsp. vanilla

For batter, combine all ingredients and beat for 4 minutes. Pour into greased bundt pan and bake at 350° for 45 minutes. Remove from pan to cool. Prepare icing by combining all ingredients. Drizzle over cake.

10-12 servings

CRANBERRY TURTLE BARS

Show ■
Go ■

Crust:
2 c. flour
½ c. light brown sugar, packed
½ tsp. salt
1¾ sticks butter, unsalted, cut into ½ inch
cubes

Topping:
2 sticks butter, unsalted
1⅔ c. sugar
¼ c. light corn syrup
½ tsp salt
1½ c. cranberries, fresh or frozen, coarsely
chopped
1 tsp vanilla
3 c. (12 oz) toasted pecans
3 oz. bittersweet chocolate, finely chopped

Crust: Put pecans in a single layer on a cookie sheet and bake at 350° for 10 minutes. Chop the pecans as soon as they have cooled. Line a 10x15-inch shallow baking pan with foil leaving 2 inches of foil over the edge. Butter foil on the sides but not the bottom. Combine flour, brown sugar and salt. Add butter and mix until it forms pea size lumps. Knead dough into a single ball. Roll dough between two sheets of waxed paper to ⅛ inch thickness. Pat dough into bottom of pan. Bake at 350° for 15-17 minutes until golden. Cool on rack.

Topping: Melt butter in a 3-qt. saucepan. Stir in sugar, corn syrup and salt. Boil over medium high heat, stirring for 8 minutes until mixture registers 245° on a candy thermometer. Stir in cranberries and boil about 5 more minutes until mixture returns to 245°. Remove from heat, stir in vanilla and pecans until well coated. Quickly spread over dough base. Cool before adding chocolate decoration.

Melt the chocolate in a double boiler. Put chocolate in a small ziplock bag and cut off a corner to drizzle over the top of the bars. Refrigerate until cold. Remove from pan by pulling on the sides of aluminum foil. Cut into pieces. To store bars: separate layers with plastic wrap.

48-64 servings

APPLE CRISP

Show ☐
Go ■

5 c. apples, peeled and sliced
1 c. sugar
1 tsp. cinnamon
1 T. flour, heaping

Topping:
½ c. flour
¾ c. quick oatmeal
½ tsp. baking powder
¼ tsp. baking soda
¾ c. brown sugar
⅓ c. butter, cold, cut into cubes

Mix first four ingredients and put in greased 8x8-inch pan. For topping, combine dry ingredients in a food processor. Add butter pieces and pulse until texture is coarse. Sprinkle over fruit. Bake at 350° for 40-45 minutes or until apples are done. Serve warm with ice cream.

6 servings

RHUBARB CRUMBLE

Show ☐
Go ■

Crumble:
1 c. flour
¾ c. quick oatmeal
1 c. brown sugar
½ c. butter, cold, cut into cubes
1 tsp. cinnamon

Filling:
4 c. rhubarb, cut into ½ inch pieces
1 c. sugar
1 c. water
1 tsp. vanilla
2 T. cornstarch

Blend first five ingredients in food processor until clumps appear. Do not over blend. Spread ¾ of mixture in lightly greased 8x8-inch pan. Sprinkle rhubarb pieces over bottom. Mix sugar, water, vanilla and cornstarch in saucepan. Cook on medium heat until liquid is clear. Pour over rhubarb. Top with remaining crumble. Bake at 350° for 45 minutes.

6 servings

Other Good Stuff

STEAK MARINADE

Show ■
Go ☐

1 T. red wine vinegar
2 T. ketchup
3 T. oil
3 T. soy sauce
¼ tsp. pepper
1 clove garlic, crushed

Mix all ingredients and pour over meat. Marinate at least 3 hours or overnight.

½ cup

PESTO SAUCE

Show ■
Go ■

2 c. fresh basil leaves
½ c. olive oil
2 T. pignoli (pine nuts)
2 cloves garlic, crushed
1 tsp. salt
½ c. freshly grated parmesan cheese
2 T. freshly grated Romano cheese
3 T. butter, softened

In a blender or food processor mix together the basil, oil, pine nuts, garlic, salt and cheeses; then add the butter.

2¾ cups

MAYONNAISE

Show ■
Go ■

1 egg
1 tsp. fresh lemon juice
1 tsp. red wine vinegar
1-2 tsp. Dijon mustard
1 tsp. salt
freshly ground white pepper
1¼ c. safflower oil
¼ c. olive oil

In food processor or blender, mix egg, lemon juice, vinegar, mustard, salt and pepper. Combine oils. Add 3 tablespoons to egg mixture. Process for 5 seconds. With motor running, add remaining oil in a steady stream until mayonnaise thickens. When thick add remaining oil quickly.

1½ cups

MUSHROOM SAUCE

Show ■
Go ■

4½ T. butter
8 oz. fresh mushrooms, sliced
3 T. flour
¾ c. milk
¾ c. whipping cream
salt to taste
pepper to taste
⅛ tsp. nutmeg
1 c. shredded Swiss cheese
1 egg yolk
¼ c. dry white wine

In small skillet, melt 2 tablespoons butter and sauté mushrooms 4 minutes. Set aside. In medium saucepan, melt remaining 2½ tablespoons butter. Blend in flour and gradually stir in milk and cream. Bring to a boil. Season with salt and pepper and nutmeg. Stir in cheese until melted. Beat egg yolk with wine and add to mixture. Cook 1 minute, add mushrooms and reheat a few minutes.

3½ cups

FRESH HERB BUTTER

Show ■
Go ■

½ c. finely chopped fresh parsley
½ c. finely chopped fresh dill
2 marjoram leaves, chopped
4 green onions, finely chopped
1 tsp. lemon balm or verbena (optional)
1 lb. butter, margarine or cream cheese,
    softened
¼ tsp. salt
¼ tsp. pepper
¼ tsp. crushed garlic

Blend herbs and butter. Add salt, pepper and garlic. Place in crock and store in refrigerator. Serve on homemade bread, potatoes, vegetables, steak or chicken.

1 pound

Fresh herbs are a must.

SWEET DILL MUSTARD

Show ■
Go ■

1 c. dry mustard
1 c. cider vinegar
¾ c. sugar
¼ c. water
2 tsp. salt
1½ tsp. dill weed
2 eggs, slightly beaten

In a small bowl, combine mustard, vinegar, sugar, water, salt and dill weed. Let stand at room temperature 4-6 hours. Stir in eggs. Cook mixture in double boiler about 8-10 minutes, stirring occasionally. Cool, cover and refrigerate at least 24 hours before using. If mustard is too thick, thin with white wine.

2 cups

SHALLOT BUTTER

Show ■
Go ■

4½ oz. shallots
4½ oz. butter, softened

In hot water, blanch shallots, quickly drain and squeeze well in cloth. Chop until fine. Add butter and mix. For a finer texture, press through sieve.

¼ cup

PICKLES FOREVER

Show ■
Go ☐

8 thinly sliced cucumbers (peeled or unpeeled)
1½ c. thinly sliced onions
1½ T. salt
1 c. sliced celery
1 green pepper, sliced
2 c. sugar
1 c. white vinegar
1½ tsp. mustard seed
1 tsp. celery seed

Combine cucumbers, onions, salt, celery and green pepper; let stand 30 minutes. Drain off liquid. Mix sugar, vinegar, mustard seed and celery seed together; add to cucumber mixture. Refrigerate. More vegetables may be added as needed.

10 cups

SPICED GREEN PEPPER JELLY

Show ■
Go ■

3 lg. green peppers, seeded and finely chopped
½ c. white vinegar
6½ c. sugar
3 T. crushed dry red pepper flakes
2 (3 oz.) pkgs. Certo
5 drops green food coloring

In medium saucepan, combine peppers, vinegar, sugar and red pepper; bring to a rolling boil. Add Certo and return to a boil. Skim green foam and continue boiling for 2 minutes. Add coloring and skim again. Pour in small jars; cover and refrigerate. Serve spread on block of cream cheese, with snack bread or crackers.

10 cups

THE PLANNER'S GINGERY PLUM CHUTNEY

Show ■
Go ☐

1 c. sugar
1 c. light brown sugar, firmly packed
¾ c. cider vinegar
1½ tsp. crushed red pepper flakes
2 tsp. salt
2 tsp. mustard seed
3 cloves garlic, crushed
¼ c. grated onion
½ c. thinly sliced preserved ginger and juice
1 c. golden raisins
1 qt. fresh Italian prune plums

Cook all ingredients except plums in Dutch oven (or crockpot turned to 300°) over high heat, stirring occasionally until sugar is dissolved. Halve and pit plums and add to Dutch oven. Cover. Turn heat to low (crockpot to 200°) and cook 2-3 hours. (It will take 4-6 hours in a crockpot but needs very little watching). Stir occasionally. Can remove cover and cook down to desired consistency. Ladle into hot sterilized jars and seal. (If kept in refrigerator canning jars are not necessary.)

3 pints

Wonderful hostess gifts!

CARAMEL NUT SAUCE

Show ■
Go ■

½ c. brown sugar, packed
½ c. light corn syrup
2 T. butter
¼ tsp. salt
¾ c. chopped toasted pecans
¼ c. whipping cream
1 tsp. vanilla

Combine sugar, syrup, butter and salt in medium saucepan. Stir over medium heat until sugar is dissolved. Remove from heat. Stir in nuts, cream and vanilla. Serve hot over ice cream.

2 cups

CARAMEL SAUCE

Show ■
Go ☐

1¼ c. sugar
½ c. butter
1 c. whipping cream

In heavy skillet, over very low heat, cook sugar until brown. Watch carefully to avoid burning. Do not stir, but frequently shake pan. It will take 30-40 minutes for sugar to turn to a brown liquid. Stir in butter. When butter is melted, it will be separated on top of sugar. Over low heat, with wooden spoon, blend in cream, stirring constantly until mixture is smooth. Sauce may be stored in covered container in refrigerator up to 1 week. Before serving, heat sauce in top of double boiler. Serve as a topping for ice cream.

2 cups

HOT FUDGE SAUCE

Show ■
Go ■

1 c. sugar
3 T. flour
¼ tsp. salt
1¼ c. milk
2 (1 oz.) sq. unsweetened chocolate (or 2 packets of pre-melted chocolate)

Combine dry ingredients in saucepan; add milk and chocolate. Cook over medium heat stirring frequently until chocolate melts and ingredients come to a boil. Sauce will thicken as it cooks. Remove from heat and serve. If sauce is too thick, slowly add a little warm milk, stirring until proper consistency is reached. Also can be reheated, uncovered, in the microwave for 1-2 minutes depending on the amount left. A few drops of peppermint flavoring may be added.

1½ cups

HOT FUDGE/CARAMEL SAUCE

Show ■
Go ■

½ c. whole milk
1 lb. caramels
½ lb. semi-sweet chocolate
½ pt. vanilla ice cream, softened
1 tsp. vanilla

Heat milk and caramels in double boiler until caramels are melted. Chop chocolate and add to caramel mixture. Add ice cream and vanilla. Blend; heat and serve.

3 cups

Just a spoonful of fudge sauce makes the medicine go down.

M&M CARAMEL CORN

Show ■
Go ■

½ c. light corn syrup
1⅓ c. sugar
1 c. butter
2 qts. popped popcorn
2 c. mixed nuts
1-1½ c. M&M candies

Combine syrup, sugar and butter in medium saucepan and bring to boil. Continue boiling on low heat to hard ball stage. Combine popcorn, nuts and M&M's in a large bowl. Pour syrup over top and mix together. Spread on a greased jelly roll pan. Refrigerate until cold. Break into pieces.

3 quarts

CARAMEL PUFF-CORN

Show ■
Go ■

2 (5 oz.) bags puffcorn curls or hulless
    popped corn
1 lb. nuts (optional)
1 c. butter
2 c. brown sugar, firmly packed
½ c. light or dark corn syrup
½ tsp. baking soda
1 tsp. vanilla

Place puffcorn curls and nuts in large roasting pan. Combine butter, brown sugar and corn syrup in heavy 4 quart saucepan. Cook over medium heat, stirring until sugar is dissolved and all ingredients are mixed. Bring to a boil and boil for 5 minutes. Remove from heat; stir in baking soda and vanilla. Pour hot syrup over puffcorn, stirring to mix and coat well. Bake uncovered at 250° for 1 hour, stirring every 15 minutes. Let cool and continue to stir so it doesn't stick to pan. Store in airtight containers.

5 quarts

PEANUT CLUSTERS

Show ■
Go ■

1 lb. white almond bark
1 (12 oz.) pkg. chocolate chips
1 lb. Spanish peanuts

Melt bark and chocolate chips in double boiler or microwave. Mix in peanuts. Drop by teaspoonfuls onto waxed paper. Cool. Remove and serve plain or place in paper candy cups.

3 dozen

NUT GOODIE BAR CANDY

Show ■
Go ☐

1 (12 oz.) pkg. chocolate chips
1 (12 oz.) pkg. butterscotch chips
2 c. creamy peanut butter
1 (1 oz.) sq. unsweetened chocolate
1 c. butter
⅓ c. evaporated or ½ c. regular milk
¼ c. regular vanilla pudding mix
2 lbs. powdered sugar
1 tsp. maple flavoring
½ lb. Spanish peanuts, skinned

In double boiler or microwave, melt chips, peanut butter and chocolate. Spread half of the melted chocolate mixture in a foil-lined buttered, 10½x15½-inch jelly roll pan. Refrigerate or freeze until set (about 30 minutes in freezer). Reserve remaining chocolate mixture in double boiler.

In heavy saucepan, combine butter, milk and pudding mix. Bring to boil over low heat and cook 1 minute. Remove and let cool. Using a mixer, blend in powdered sugar and flavoring until creamy. Spread mixture over chilled chocolate. Stir Spanish peanuts into remaining chocolate mixture and spread over top. Refrigerate for 3 hours. Peel off foil and cut into 1 inch squares. Keep refrigerated.

150 pieces

GRANOLA CANDY

Show ■
Go ■

1 (12 oz.) pkg. chocolate chips
1 (12 oz.) pkg. butterscotch chips
1½ c. salted mixed nuts
1½ c. 100% natural cereal with raisins and
  dates

In double boiler, melt chocolate and butterscotch chips. Add nuts and cereal; mix well. Line a 10½x15½-inch jelly roll pan with greased waxed paper. Spread candy mixture evenly in pan and refrigerate. When set, cut or break into pieces.

20-25 pieces

ENGLISH TOFFEE

Show ■
Go ■

2 c. butter
2½ c. sugar
1½ c. whole unblanched almonds
3 c. chocolate chips
1½ c. chopped walnuts

In heavy skillet, melt butter. Add sugar and cook over moderate heat, stirring often until mixture foams vigorously. Turn heat to low; cook and stir 5 minutes longer. Add almonds and cook over medium heat until nuts begin to pop, about 10 minutes. Lower heat and cook 7 minutes, stirring occasionally. Pour into a 10½x15½-inch jelly roll pan and cool until it hardens. Melt chocolate chips and spread ½ over top of cooled candy. Sprinkle ¾ cup walnuts on top of chocolate. Cool. Flip onto board. Spread other side with remaining chocolate and walnuts. Cool and break into pieces.

40 pieces

What a way to "waist" calories!

CARAMEL NUT CANDY

Show ■
Go □

2 (12 oz.) pkgs. chocolate chips
2 lbs. assorted nuts or salted peanuts
3 c. brown sugar
1 c. butter
1 c. light corn syrup
1 (14 oz.) can sweetened condensed milk

Line sides and bottom of a 10½x15½-inch jelly roll pan with foil; butter foil. In double boiler, melt chocolate chips over low heat and spread half of it in thin layer on the foil. Sprinkle nuts over hot chocolate. Mix together sugar, butter, syrup and milk and cook very slowly until it reaches soft ball stage or 240° on a candy thermometer. Spread on top of nuts. Let cool 5 minutes. Spread remaining chocolate on top of caramel layer. Refrigerate until set. Lift out of pan and remove foil. Cut into 1 inch squares and place in paper candy cups.

150 pieces

GRANOLA

Show □
Go ■

4 c. oats
½ c. flour
½ c. wheat germ
½ c. coconut
1 tsp. cinnamon
1 tsp. vanilla
½ c. slivered almonds
¼ c. brown sugar
¼ c. honey
½ c. oil

Mix dry ingredients together. Mix vanilla, honey and oil then pour over dry ingredients. Bake 10 minutes at 350°, stir/toss well and bake another 10 minutes, or until light golden brown.

150 pieces

HOT APPLE CIDER

Show ■
Go ■

2¼ c. sugar
4 c. water
¼ tsp. ground cloves
¼ tsp. ground ginger
3 cinnamon sticks
6 T. lemon juice
2 quarts apple cider
2 (6 oz.) cans orange juice concentrate
2 quarts water

Combine sugar and 4 cups of water in a pan and cook for 10 min. Add cloves, cinnamon and ginger. Let stand 1 hour. Add lemon juice, cider, orange juice and 2 quarts water. Heat until hot. Serve with cinnamon sticks.

KALBI MARINADE

Show ☐
Go ■

½ c. sugar
½ c. oil
½ c. sesame oil
2 tsp. garlic
1 tsp. ginger
¼ tsp. red pepper
⅛ tsp. black pepper
1½ tsp. sesame seeds
3 green onions, minced

Combine ingredients, mix well and marinate beef or chicken overnight. Great marinade for grilling.

Celebrity
Chefs

SZECHUAN STIR-FRIED GREEN BEANS

TOBIE NIDETZ

Show ■
Go ■

Sauce
1 T. sugar
½ c. soy sauce
⅛ c. chicken broth, low salt
½ tsp. sesame oil, dark

2 T. peanut oil
1 whole red chile pepper
1 clove garlic
¼ c. onion, diced
3 T. pickled Szechwan Vegetable,
   julienne cut (canned, found in Asian
   grocery stores)
¾ lb. fresh green beans
¾ c. peanut oil

Combine the first four ingredients in a small bowl, set aside. Heat a large wok over high flame. Add the oil, swirl to coat bottom third of pan. Heat until oil smokes. Crush garlic clove with the side of a broad knife and add to oil. Break the chile pepper in half. Use ½ if the red chile pepper is large or all if it is small. Stir fry until garlic begins to brown. Add onion until it turns brown. Add reserved sauce and boil to reduce by ¼ volume. Heat ¾ c. oil in a high sided saucepan until temperature reaches 375° on a good fat thermometer. Make sure beans are dry. Fry beans until they appear wrinkled and slightly whitened, approximately 60 seconds. Place beans on a paper towel to drain oil. Toss beans in sauce. Serve immediately.

4 servings

KOTA STO PHYLLO (GREEK CHICKEN AND PHYLLO)

CHRISTOS GREEK RESTAURANT

Show ■
Go ■

4 (5 oz.) chicken breasts, boneless, skinless
2 lb. fresh spinach
¼ c. virgin olive oil
½ c. yellow onion, finely chopped
½ c. green onion, finely chopped
2 cloves garlic, crushed
3 T. fresh dill, chopped
5 leeks, diced
1 c. feta cheese, crumbled
¼ c. ricotta cheese
¾ lb kasseri cheese, shredded
2 eggs, lightly beaten
½ c. butter, melted
12 sheets phyllo dough
salt and pepper, to taste

Wash and stem spinach; drain thoroughly and cut into ¼ inch lengths. Heat oil in a large skillet. Add onions, leeks, garlic and dill; sauté 2-3 minutes. Add spinach and sauté until moisture has evaporated. Season with salt and pepper. Let sauté mix cool completely. Add eggs and cheese; mix thoroughly by hand. Pound chicken breasts out to flatten; season with salt and pepper. Create three 1 oz. balls out of the finished filling mix. Set aside. Lay pounded chicken breast down and place a ball of filling over it. Roll chicken breast around the filling. Set aside. Lay one sheet of phyllo dough flat on a work surface. Brush phyllo lightly with melted butter working from the edge to the center. Lay a second sheet of phyllo over the first, again buttering lightly. Repeat a third time. Lay a roll of chicken breast with filling at the center of each phyllo half. Fold the ends over the chicken, then fold in the sides and tightly roll the ball away from you. Brush the rolls lightly with butter and place seam side down on an ungreased baking sheet. Repeat the process until the batch of filling is used up. Bake on a baking sheet, at least one inch apart, in preheated oven at 400° until golden (25-30 minutes). Use plunge thermometer to ensure 145° temperature at core.

4 servings

SHIRRED EGGS WITH SPINACH AND CROUTONS

Show ■
Go ■

LUCIA'S RESTAURANT
CHEF LUCIA WATSON

2 (12 oz.) ramekins
1 T. butter
1 c. cream
2 cloves garlic, chopped
1 tsp. fresh thyme, chopped
1 tsp. rosemary, chopped
1 c. bread, cubed crouton size
2 T. olive oil
salt and pepper
1 c. spinach, washed
4 eggs

Generously butter the ramekins and preheat oven to 400°. Put the cream on the stove with half the garlic, half the herbs and some salt and pepper. Bring to a boil, then reduce the heat to a simmer. Let cook for about 4-5 minutes or until reduced by half. Taste the cream, it should be well seasoned. Set aside.

Make the croutons: Toss the cubed bread in the olive oil, the rest of the garlic cloves, salt and pepper. Toss thoroughly together. In a hot skillet, fry the bread until crispy and browned, about 5 minutes. Taste for seasoning and set aside. Put about a fistful of the spinach into each buttered ramekin. Break two eggs on top of the spinach. Place half the croutons on top, then ladle cream over to just cover everything. Bake the eggs for about 12-15 minutes (depending on how soft you like your eggs), and serve at once.

2 servings

PAN SEARED CHICKEN BREAST WITH BUTTERNUT SQUASH

Show ■
Go ■

GUSTO CAFE
CHEF CHARLES A. VENABLES

2 (8 oz.) chicken breasts (skin-on with wing bone attached)
2 c. butternut squash, diced into ¼ inch pieces
2 T. olive oil
2 c. chicken stock
¼ c. diced red pepper
2 T. fresh sage, chopped
2 T. butter

Preheat oven to 375°. Preheat sauté pan. Add olive oil. When oil is hot, add chicken breast skin-side down. Cook over high heat until golden brown. Place squash in sauté pan and roast in oven for approx. 12 min. Remove chicken from pan and let rest. Place sauté pan with squash over high heat. Add chicken stock, red pepper, sage, butter, salt and pepper to taste. Reduce for 3-5 minutes. Place sauce in a soup plate or pasta bowl. Slice chicken breast and place over sauce. This can be served with orzo or rice, if desired. This dish can be adapted to reflect the seasons. For example, you can use chopped, peeled, seeded tomatoes, artichokes and fresh tarragon.

2 servings

TURKEY OSSO BUCO

FIRELAKE RESTAURANT AT
RADISSON PLAZA
EXECUTIVE CHEF PAUL LYNCH

Show ■
Go ■

6 large turkey legs

Rub:
1½ tsp. smoked paprika
1½ tsp. coriander, ground
1½ tsp. cumin, ground
⅜ tsp. cinnamon
⅜ tsp. allspice, ground
⅛ tsp. cayenne pepper
pinch of salt

Sauté:
¾ c. onion, diced
8¼ T. fresh ginger, grated
1½ T. garlic, minced
⅜ tsp red pepper, crushed

Deglaze:
⅜ c. apple cider
1½ T. tomato paste
1½ cinnamon sticks

Add & Braise:
1½ c. tomato, diced
¾ c. chicken stock
1½ bay leaves
1½ T. honey
¾ c. oranges, peeled and quartered

Add after 2 hours:
¾ c. chickpeas
¾ c. raisins, Craisins, figs or dates (chop the figs or dates)

Mix the rub ingredients together and rub on turkey legs. Place sauté ingredients in a large pan and place turkey legs on top. Sauté until brown. Remove legs and add deglazing ingredients. Add all but the chickpeas and raisins. Replace turkey legs. Cover and braise in a 325° oven for 3 hours. Add the last two ingredients after two hours. When done, remove the tendons with fish pliers. Serve with Almond Pearl Couscous.

6 servings

ALMOND PEARL COUSCOUS

Show ■
Go ■

⅓ c. onion, diced
1 T. olive oil
¹⁄₁₆ tsp. allspice
⅓ tsp. cinnamon
1 c. pearl couscous
1¾ c. chicken stock
⅓ c. dried apricots, diced
salt, to taste
⅓ c. slivered almonds, toasted

In a heavy bottomed pan, sauté onion, allspice and cinnamon in olive oil. Add couscous, stock and salt. Bring to a boil. Reduce heat and cover for 10 minutes. Remove from heat and let rest for 5 minutes. Add the almonds and apricots and fluff before serving.

6 servings

WHITE BEAN AND SQUASH SOUP

Show ■
Go ■

SPOON RIVER/CAFE BRENDA
BRENDA LANGDON

1 c. dried navy beans
5 c. water
1 T. olive oil
4 cloves garlic, chopped
1 large shallot, chopped
1 med. onion, chopped
3½ c. winter squash, peeled and cubed in
    1 inch pieces
½ tsp dried basil
½ tsp. dried oregano
¼ tsp. dried thyme
4 c. vegetable stock
salt and pepper, to taste
¾ c. half and half or soy milk (optional)

Wash beans and cover with 5 cups water in a large pot. Bring to a boil, reduce heat and simmer, covered, for approximately 1½ hours or until beans are tender. Drain. In a soup pot, sauté garlic, shallot, and onion in 1 T. olive oil for 5 min. Add cubed squash, cooked beans, herbs and stock. Bring to a boil, then reduce the heat and simmer, covered until squash is tender, approximately 20 minutes. Puree soup in batches in blender. Return to soup pot, add half and half or soy milk, and taste to adjust seasoning. Add salt and pepper to taste.

6 servings

CHICKEN GORGONZOLA CROSTINI

FRENCH MEADOW BAKERY
LYNN GORDON

Show ■
Go ■

4 slices organic pan levain, pan campagne
    or baguette, sliced long diagonally;
    cut ½ inch thick.
3 T. organic extra virgin olive oil
garlic cloves, organic, peeled and cut in
    half (optional)

Topping:
2 free range chicken breasts, grilled
8 oz. Gorgonzola cheese
8 oz. cream cheese, organic
½ c. walnuts, organic, toasted and chopped
½ c. green onions, organic, finely sliced
½ c. dried cranberries, organic

Cut grilled chicken breast in small ¼ inch pieces. Add walnuts, green onions and cranberries; set aside. Blend Gorgonzola cheese and softened cream cheese with a fork or hand mixer until smooth and soft. Gently fold chicken mixture into softened cheese. Set aside. Brush olive oil on both sides of bread and arrange on a cookie sheet. Place bread in a 400° oven until bread is lightly golden but not hard toasted all the way through. If desired, rub one side of toast with the cut clove of garlic. Spread cheese mixture on each toast then return to oven and broil for 1 minute, or until cheese bubbles.

6 servings

IKE'S HAMBURGER SEASONING

IKE'S CHIP ISSACSON

Show ■
Go ■

¾ c. Lowry's seasoning
½ c. sugar
3 T. granulated garlic
3 T. onion powder
3 T. white pepper

Blend and sprinkle liberally on steaks, chops or burgers before grilling.

6 servings

JACK'S POTATO KNISHES

IT TAKES THE CAKE
JACK LEBOW

Show ■
Go ■

5 lbs. baking potatoes, baked until soft, then peeled warm (6 large russets)
2 lbs. onions (3 cups) peeled, diced and sautéed in vegetable oil until caramelized
1 T. salt
1 T. freshly ground pepper
¾ c. chicken-flavored cooking stock
2 pkgs. Pepperidge Farm Puff Pastry (4 sheets), room temperature
vegetable oil or schmaltz for basting

For potato mixture beat ingredients until desired texture. Season to taste. Open pastry sheets and roll out to approximately 13x15-inch diameter. Cut dough in half, and using a 1½-inch ice cream scoop, place 5 scoops of filling in center of each sheet. Place a small amount of water on edge of dough. Fold dough over potato mixture and press to seal. With side of hand, press into dough between each section that was created by the scoop (about every three inches or so) and then cut through with a knife. Twist both ends of potato filled dough and tuck in center. Place knishes on parchment-lined baking sheets at least two inches apart. Repeat with remaining filling and dough and baste with oil or schmaltz. Bake at 350° for 20-25 minutes until golden brown.

Makes approximately 42 pieces.

CHICKEN CAESAR PASTA SALAD

CAFE LATTE
LINDA QUINN

Show ■
Go ■

2 chicken breasts, boneless and skinless
1 (1 lb.) pkg. extra-wide pasta noodles, cooked
1 head Romaine, chopped into 2-inch pieces
1 red onion, chopped
2 (½ lb.) pkgs. mushrooms, sliced thin
1 c. grated parmesan cheese

Dressing:
1 T. anchovy paste
½ c. fresh garlic, chopped
3 T. white wine vinegar
2 T. Dijon mustard
1 tsp. salt
1 tsp. black pepper
¼ c. lemon juice
1 c. olive oil
½ c. vegetable oil

Grill chicken breasts until done. Slice or cube into bite-sized pieces. After pasta has been cooked, cool under cold running water, drain well. In a large bowl, mix the chicken, pasta, Romaine, onion, mushrooms and parmesan cheese. Using a hand mixer, combine the anchovy paste, garlic, wine vinegar, mustard, salt, pepper and lemon juice; blend together until garlic is pureed. Slowly drizzle oils in while still mixing. Pour over salad and mix well.

8-10 servings

ARTICHOKE DIP

LORING CAFE

Show ■
Go ■

1 can artichokes, drained
½ clove garlic, crushed
½ c. mayonnaise
2 T. pimento, diced, heaping
½ c. parmesan cheese
¼ c. Swiss cheese, shredded
¼ tsp. cayenne pepper
breadcrumbs
salt, to taste

Mix together in glass pie plate or other similar sized dish. Sprinkle crushed bread crumbs on top. Bake at 400° for 20 minutes. Do not over bake. Serve with crackers of your choice.

8-10 servings

FAMOUS TABLESIDE GUACAMOLE RECIPE

Show ■
Go ■

TEJAS RESTAURANT
MARK HAUGEN

4 avocados, pitted and peeled
1 lg. tomato, diced into ¼ inch squares
1 sm. onion, diced into ¼ inch pieces
2 T. cilantro, chopped
2 Serrano chiles, minced
1 lime, juiced
4 dashes Tabasco
2 dashes Worcestershire
4 cloves roasted garlic
1 tsp. salt

Mix and serve.

6 servings

FABULOUS FUDGE BARS

Show ■
Go ■

BREAD AND CHOCOLATE
CHEF LINDA QUINN

Dough:
1 c. butter, room temperature
2 c. brown sugar
2 eggs
4 c. old fashioned-oatmeal
2 c. flour
2 tsp. baking soda
1 tsp. salt

Fudge center:
3 T. butter
1-14 oz. can sweetened condensed milk
2 c. chopped chocolate (good quality), melted
1 c. pecans, chopped
1 tsp. vanilla

In a mixing bowl, cream butter and brown sugar. Add eggs and beat well. In a medium bowl, combine oatmeal, flour, baking soda and salt. Add to butter mixture until combined. In a small saucepan, melt butter and condensed milk on low heat. When it is warm, add melted chocolate, pecans and vanilla. Press ⅓ of the dough mixture in the bottom of a 9x13-inch pan. Top with fudge mixture. Crumble remaining oat mixture on top. Bake at 350° for 20-25 minutes.

4–6 servings

RATATOUILLE

PATRICK'S BISTRO – WAYZATA
PATRICK BERNET

Show ■
Go ■

2 T. extra-virgin olive oil
2 onions, small & chopped
2 eggplant, cubed small
4 garlic cloves, minced
2 zucchini, cubed small
1 red bell pepper, seeded and cubed
1 yellow bell pepper, seeded and cubed
10 ripe tomatoes, blanched, seeded and
    coarsely chopped
4 fresh thyme sprigs
1 dried bay leaf
½ tsp. salt
½ tsp. freshly ground pepper
¼ c. minced fresh basil

In a large saucepan over medium heat, warm the olive oil. When it is hot, reduce heat to medium low. Add the onions and sauté 2 minutes until translucent. Add the eggplant and garlic and sauté, stirring often for 3-4 minutes. You may need to add more oil. Add the zucchini and bell peppers for 4-5 minutes more. Add the tomatoes, thyme, bay leaf, salt and pepper. Stir and turn for 2-3 more minutes. Cover, reduce heat to low and cook for 40 minutes, stirring occasionally until vegetables are soft and blended together. Stir in the basil and remove from the heat. Transfer to a serving bowl and serve hot or cold.

8 servings

VANILLA CRÈME FRAICHE WITH MIXED BERRIES (SEMI-ICE CREAM)

DAVID FHIMA

Show ■
Go ■

Note: must be prepared 48 hours before serving.

Approximately 20 oz. mixed berries of your
    preference
1 quart heavy cream
1 T. lemon juice
1 c. buttermilk
2 T. vanilla extract
½ c. honey

To heavy cream add lemon juice, buttermilk, vanilla extract and honey. Mix well and let stand covered at room temperature for 36 hours (Yes, 36 hours!). Uncover and whisk gently. Add mixed berries. Pour into individual small parfait glasses for serving and freeze overnight.

8-10 servings

POTATO PANCAKES

ANDREW ZIMMERN

Show ■
Go ■

3 lg. russet potatoes
3 med. Yukon Gold potatoes, peeled,
   cooked and riced
2 eggs, beaten
2 tsp. sea salt
½ tsp. ground white pepper
½ c. matzo meal
1 lg. yellow onion, grated
2 c. apple sauce
1 c. sour cream

Smoked salmon-dill-creme fraiche:
½ c. creme fraiche
dill to taste
½ lb. sliced Smoked salmon
(combine above three ingredients)

Peel and grate the russet potatoes. Rinse with cold water; drain. Gently press to remove excess water. Mix half the potatoes with the riced (mashed) potatoes. Pulse the other half of the grated potatoes with the onion in the food processor to form a paste. Do not overwork. Combine the two mixtures, season with salt, pepper, eggs and matzo meal. Heat enough vegetable oil in a large skillet over medium heat so that it comes up the sides of the pan ¼-inch. When oil is 350° or batter sizzles, fry small 2-3 inch size patties in batches until golden brown on both sides. Drain on paper towels. Serve, garnishing with apple sauce and sour cream on half the cakes, and smoked salmon-dill-creme fraiche on the others.

Approximately 4 dozen

FRESH POTATO AND SMOKED SALMON SALAD

JENNY BREEN

Show ■
Go ■

8 medium red or yellow potatoes, cut into
    1 inch pieces
1 c. sun-dried tomatoes, cut into pieces
    and softened in hot water
12 oz. smoked salmon, broken into large
    pieces
¼ c. olive oil
¼ c. cider vinegar
1 tsp. salt
¼-⅓ c. mayonnaise, regular or soy
2 T. Dijon mustard
4 cloves garlic, minced
2 medium leeks
½ lb. spinach
¼ c. basil leaves, chopped or 2 T. dry basil

Boil potatoes until soft. Combine potatoes, tomatoes, 2 tablespoons of the oil, vinegar, salt, mayonnaise and mustard. Heat the other 2 tablespoons oil and sauté garlic and leeks. When these are soft, add basil and spinach for 30 seconds. Remove from heat. Add to other ingredients and mix well. Add salmon last. Chill until ready to serve.

8 servings

TOMATO ORANGE GINGER BROTH

FIVE STAR

CHEF SID LARSON

Show ■
Go ■

2 quarts chicken stock (consommé
    preferred)
1 c. orange juice, plus zest from 4 oranges
2 T. tomato paste
6 ripe tomatoes, peeled, seeded, julienned

Syrup:
1 tsp ginger, peeled and sliced
2 T. sugar
2 oz. water

Simmer ginger, sugar and water for 5 minutes. Add syrup with rest of ingredients. Simmer for 30 minutes. Adjust seasoning with salt and pepper. Blend thoroughly in blender. Garnish with candied ginger or fresh rosemary sprigs.

8 servings

PAN-SEARED SKATE WING WITH SUNCHOKES, HAZEL NUTS AND BROWN BUTTER HOLLANDAISE
FUGAISE

Show ■
Go ■

2½ lbs. Skate wing fish fillet
flour
1 T. canola oil
2 lbs. Sunchokes (Jerusalem Artichokes)
2 strips bacon
1 onion, diced
2 c. milk
2 c. chicken stock
½ lb. Haricot Vert (green beans)
½ c. hazelnuts, toasted and chopped
2 egg yolks
1 T. water
½ lb. unsalted butter
2 T. lemon juice

Peel the sunchokes and slice ¼-inch rounds, placing them into lemon water as you go to avoid browning. Render the bacon in a pot. Add onion and two-thirds of the sliced sunchokes. Cover with chicken stock and milk and cook on low heat until sunchokes are tender. Drain all but a little bit of the liquid and puree ingredients in a blender until smooth. With the other sunchokes, cook in a little butter and chicken stock until tender, drain and reserve. Blanch the green beans in salted, boiling water for 1-2 minutes and "shock" in ice water. This helps retain green color.

For the sauce: put butter in a pan with high sides and let it boil until brown bits form on the pan. Very carefully, whisk the bits away from the pan and take off the heat. Let the butter cool slightly before adding lemon juice. Again, be very careful when adding the lemon or it may start to boil again. Keep the brown butter warm. Place egg yolks in a stainless steel bowl with the water and whisk over a simmering pot of water until thick and frothy. Slowly drizzle the browned butter into the egg yolks, whisking rapidly. Once all the butter is incorporated, season with salt, pepper and more lemon juice (optional). Keep warm but not hot.

For the fish: season with salt and pepper. Heat oil in a sauté pan until just smoking. Dust one side with flour and place in the hot oil. Place the pan directly into a 400° oven for about 3 minutes depending on the thickness of the filet. The meat should be easily pierced with a knife.

To finish: heat the sunchoke slices in a little butter with the green beans and hazelnuts. Plate the sunchoke puree and the vegetable mixture. Place the fish on top and drizzle the hollandaise over the fish.

4–6 servings

MARYLAND STYLE CRAB CAKES

THE OCEANAIRE SEAFOOD ROOM
EXECUTIVE CHEF RICK KIMMES

Show ■
Go ■

8 eggs, whole
4 c. mayonnaise
1 tsp. dry mustard
1 T. Old Bay Seasoning
¼ bunch parsley, chopped
1 small onion, chopped
4 lbs. jumbo lump crab meat
1-1½ lb. loaf Pullman loaf bread (white bread)
4 oz. butter
2 tsp. Old Bay Seasoning
Mustard Mayonnaise or tartar sauce

In a large mixing bowl mix the first six ingredients, chill. Remove crust from Pullman loaf and cut into small cubes. Open crab and inspect for cartilage or shell; drain. In another large mixing bowl add the bread cubes and ½ of the dressing, mixing well. You may need to add more dressing. Add crab to mixture gently. The mixture should hold its shape when formed into a ball. If it is loose, add more dressing. Form into small cakes (4-5 oz.) for entree size or 1 oz. cakes for appetizer. Place cakes on a greased cookie sheet, top with a small amount of butter seasoned with Old Bay, and place in a 400° oven for 10-12 minutes until golden brown. Serve with Mustard Mayonnaise or your favorite tartar sauce (mayonnaise, dry mustard, Dijon Mustard, Worcestershire Sauce and salt, thinned with a small amount of cream).

8-10 servings

TARRAGON CHICKEN SALAD

YUM! KITCHEN AND BAKERY
CHEF MIKE GROSSMAN

Show ■
Go ■

butter for pan
1 yellow onion , thinly sliced
6 sprigs each of parsley, tarragon and
    thyme
2 bay leaves
8 large boneless, skinless chicken breast
    halves
juice of 1 lemon
1 T. kosher salt
1 T. freshly ground black pepper
1 tsp. salt
⅛ tsp. pepper
1 tsp. fresh tarragon
¼ c. sour cream
¼ c. mayonnaise
1 c. celery, diced
¾ c. pecans, chopped
½ c. grapes, sliced

Preheat oven to 375 degrees. Butter a sheet pan generously. Scatter onion slices and herbs in pan. Lay chicken breasts on top in a single layer. Sprinkle with lemon juice, salt and pepper. Cover with aluminum foil and bake for 30-40 minutes. Cool and cut into cubes. Put in a bowl and mix with salt, pepper and tarragon. Mix sour cream and mayonnaise together. Stir into chicken cubes a little at a time until creamy but not wet. Add celery, pecans and grapes. YUM!

4–6 servings

CAESAR SALAD
D'AMICO AND SONS

Show ■
Go ■

Caesar Salad
1½ lbs. chopped Romaine lettuce
salt and fresh ground pepper
½ of a lemon
3 T. grated Pecorino Romano cheese
croutons (preferably homemade)
anchovies (optional)

Dressing
1 oz. (5-6 large cloves) garlic, chopped fine
1 (2 oz.) tin anchovy filets, drained
2 T. fresh lemon juice
2 T. red wine vinegar (6-7% acid content)
1 egg
1½ tsp. Worcestershire sauce
1 T. Dijon mustard
2 T. water
½ tsp. black pepper
2 c. canola oil (or any neutral tasting
     vegetable oil)
3-4 T. water (to thin if needed)
5 T. grated Pecorino Romano cheese

Place the chopped romaine into a large, deep bowl and squeeze juice of the lemon over the lettuce. Add a couple pinches of salt and pepper to taste. Sprinkle on the grated Romano cheese and then add the Caesar dressing. Mix everything together carefully, but well, and divide evenly onto plates. Garnish with croutons and enjoy!

4–6 servings

For the dressing: Combine all of the ingredients in a deep bowl. Using a blender or food processor, blend everything together well to make the base for the dressing. With the blender of food processor running, add the oil to the base in a slow and steady stream. If the dressing is too thick at this point, blend in some or all of the water. Fold in the grated Romano cheese. Keeps up to one week in a covered container in the refrigerator.

Yields about 1 quart

BING CROSBY'S WALDORF SALAD
AS FEATURED IN DIABLO MAGAZINE

Show ■
Go ■

Dressing:

1 c. mayonnaise
1 T. lemon zest
2 T. lemon juice
salt and pepper, to taste

Salad:

2 Granny Smith apples, peeled, cored and
   thinly sliced
1 c. chopped celery
1 c. diced radishes
1 c. chopped red onions
1 c. dried cranberries (Craisins)
½ c. candied walnuts
1 c. chopped watercress
6 radicchio leaves
1 c. Maytag blue cheese crumbles

In a small bowl, mix mayonnaise, lemon zest and lemon juice. Season to taste with salt and pepper. Refrigerate while you prepare salad ingredients. Toss apples, celery, radish, Craisins and red onion with dressing to coat. Fold in watercress and candied walnuts. Place a radicchio leaf on each plate. Spoon salad onto radicchio leaf center and top with blue cheese.

6 servings

CHICKEN CORN CHOWDER

CROSSROAD DELICATESSEN

SCOTT HILL

Show ■
Go ■

½ c. butter
1 c. flour
2 T. vegetable oil
1 c. celery, diced ¼ inch thick
1½ c. onion, diced
¼ tsp. black pepper
¼ tsp. thyme leaves
1 tsp. garlic, minced
7 c. chicken broth
1 (14 oz) can cream-style corn
1 (16 oz) package frozen kernel corn
3 c. cooked potatoes, ½-inch diced
1 c. heavy cream
2 c. cooked chicken, ½-inch diced
⅓ c. roasted red peppers or pimentos,
    ¼-inch diced
salt and pepper, to taste

In a small pan, combine the flour and butter and cook to make a roux, remove from heat. In a large soup pot, add vegetable oil, celery, onion, pepper, thyme and garlic and sauté over medium heat until onions are transparent. Add broth, corn(s) and potatoes and bring to a boil. Add the roux to thicken and reduce the heat to simmer for ten minutes. Add the cream, chicken and pimentos. Increase heat to boil, adjust seasoning to taste, remove from heat and serve.

10-12 servings

Show ■
Go ■

BLINI'S WITH CAVIAR AND CUCUMBER DILL DRESSING

THE DECO CATERING
SOILE ANDERSON

4 c. milk
10 large eggs
2 tsp. salt
2 c. Rye Sourdough Starter (recipe follows)
4 c. all-purpose flour
1 c. rye flour
3 T. unsalted butter (room temp)
3½ c. salmon roe
Cucumber Dill Dressing (recipe follows)

Rye Sourdough Starter:
1 tsp. dry yeast
1 c. warm water
2 c. buttermilk, room temperature
2 T. sugar
1¾ c. rye flour

Cucumber Dill Dressing:
2 cucumbers, seeded and cut into
　　¼-inch dice
2 c. mayonnaise
2 c. sour cream
1 small onion, finely diced
1 large garlic clove, finely chopped
¼ c. fresh dill, finely chopped
1 tsp. freshly ground pepper
½ c. white vinegar

In a large bowl, whisk together milk, eggs, and salt. Add sourdough starter and flours, and whisk until mixture is well combined. Cover with kitchen towel and let stand for 1 hour. Heat griddle or large cast-iron skillet over medium heat. Brush bottom of pan with ½ teaspoon butter. Working in batches, ladle about ¼ cup batter (enough to make 4 inch pancakes) onto pan, being careful not to overcrowd: cook until bubbles form on the surface and underside is golden brown, about 1 minute more. Transfer to large ovenproof plate or baking sheet, repeat with remaining batches, adding ½ teaspoon butter to pan before each. If desired, place finished batches in a warm oven. Serve hot, with salmon roe and cucumber dill dressing on the side.

54 servings

In large mixing bowl, combine yeast and water, let stand until yeast is dissolved and bubbles form on the surface, about 5 minutes. Stir in buttermilk, sugar, and 1½ cups flour. Cover with a kitchen towel and let stand in a warm place for 24 hours. Whisk in another ¼ cup flour until well combined. Cover and set aside for another 24 hours before using or store in a jar or airtight container.

Makes 3¼ cups

For dressing, combine all ingredients in large bowl. Cover with plastic wrap and place in refrigerator until well chilled.

Makes 6 cups

Once it is nicely fermented, the dough can be stored in the refrigerator indefinitely, as long as it is replenished every 2 weeks by adding equal parts flour and water.

TOMATO AND ARUGULA SALAD WITH SMOKED BACON AND BUTTERMILK DRESSING
MISSION AND VIA RESTAURANTS
ANOUSH ANSARI

Show ■
Go ■

4 Bushel Boy tomatoes, cored, sliced in half to stack
2 oz. arugula leaves
8 slices apple wood smoked bacon, cooked
1 c. Buttermilk Dressing
2 T. fresh dill leaves
salt and pepper, to taste

Buttermilk dressing:
½ c. buttermilk
¾ c. mayonnaise
¼ tsp. red wine vinegar
1 pinch dried oregano
1 pinch Kosher salt

Combine ingredients for dressing; mix well. Evenly divide the arugula leaves between 4 chilled plates. Place one half of the tomato in the middle of the arugula, lightly salt the tomato. Add the 2 slices of bacon to form an X. Place the other half of the tomato on top of the bacon strips with the larger half of the tomato facing up. Pour 2 ounces of the buttermilk dressing over each of the tomato-bacon combinations. Confetti the dill over the entire dish.

4 servings

IRISH SODA BREAD

Show ■
Go ■

DOVER RESTAURANT
CHEF CHRIS DWYER

4 c. flour
1 tsp. baking powder
1 tsp. baking soda
1 tsp. salt
1 tsp. grated orange zest
2 T. Caraway seeds
¼ c. butter, softened
1 c. Craisins
1¼ c. buttermilk/sour milk
1 egg beaten with 2 T. milk
1 tsp. honey

Preheat oven to 325°. Grease cookie sheet. In a large bowl, sift and combine flour, baking powder and baking soda. Add salt, orange zest and caraway seeds. Cut in butter until mixture resembles coarse crumbs. Stir in Craisins and set aside. In medium bowl, mix the honey and buttermilk. Stir into the dry ingredients until they are moist. Turn out onto floured surface; knead for one minute, cut and shape. Make a cut across the top of the loaves. Brush loaves with egg wash. Let stand 10 minutes before baking. Bake for 60-75 minutes. Test by tapping the bottom of the loaves, it should sound hollow.

4–6 servings

THINGS TO KNOW

Abbreviations

tsp. = teaspoon
T. = tablespoon
c. = cup
pt. = pint
qt. = quart
oz. = ounce
lg. = large
med. = medium
lb. = pound
gal. = gallon
sq. = square
pkg. = package

Weights and Measures

3 tsp. = 1 T.
2 T. = 1 fluid oz.
4 T. = ¼ c.
5⅓ T. = ⅓ c.
8 T. = ½ c.
16 T. = 1 c.
1 lb. = 16 oz.
1 c. = ½ pt.
2 c. = 1 pt.
4 c. = 1 qt.
4 qt. = 1 gal.

Substitutions and Equivalents

2 T. butter = 1 oz.
4 T. butter = ¼ c.
1 c. butter = ½ lb.
2 c. butter = 1 lb.
2 c. sugar = 1 lb.
2¼ c. packed brown sugar = 1 lb.
1⅓ c. packed brown sugar = 1 c.
   granulated sugar
3½ c. powdered sugar = 1 lb.
4 c. sifted all purpose = 1 lb.
4½ c. sifted cake flour = 1 lb.
1 oz. chocolate = 1 sq.
3 T. cocoa & 1 T. fat = 1 oz. chocolate
1 c. egg whites = 8-10 whites
1 c. egg yolks = 12-14 yolks
25 marshmallows = ¼ lb.
1 T. cornstarch = 2 T. flour for thickening
1 T. vinegar or lemon juice &
   1 c. milk = 1 c. sour milk
10 graham crackers = 1 c. fine crumbs
1 c. whipping cream = 2 c. whipped
1 lemon = 3-4 T. juice
1 orange = 6-8 T. juice
1 c. uncooked rice = 3-4 c. cooked rice

INDEX

FOOD FOR SHOW
food on the go!
THE NEXT GENERATION

Cookbook/Sholom Home Auxiliary
3610 Phillips Parkway
St. Louis Park, MN 55426
(952) 939-1620

Please send me _____copies at **$25.60 ea.** ($24.00 per book plus $1.60 tax) _____

Add postage & handling at **$3.00 ea.** _____

TOTAL $ _____

NAME

ADDRESS

CITY   STATE   ZIP

Please make checks payable to: Cookbook/Sholom Home Auxiliary
All proceeds from sale of cookbook will benefit Mount Sinai Community Foundation and Sholom Home
Auxiliary. For gifts, please include cards and a list of addresses. **Order online: www.sholom.com**

FOOD FOR SHOW
food on the go!
THE NEXT GENERATION

Cookbook/Sholom Home Auxiliary
3610 Phillips Parkway
St. Louis Park, MN 55426
(952) 939-1620

Please send me _____copies at **$25.60 ea.** ($24.00 per book plus $1.60 tax) _____

Add postage & handling at **$3.00 ea.** _____

TOTAL $ _____

NAME

ADDRESS

CITY   STATE   ZIP

Please make checks payable to: Cookbook/Sholom Home Auxiliary
All proceeds from sale of cookbook will benefit Mount Sinai Community Foundation and Sholom Home
Auxiliary. For gifts, please include cards and a list of addresses. **Order online: www.sholom.com**

FOOD FOR SHOW
food on the go!
THE NEXT GENERATION

Cookbook/Sholom Home Auxiliary
3610 Phillips Parkway
St. Louis Park, MN 55426
(952) 939-1620

Please send me _____copies at **$25.60 ea.** ($24.00 per book plus $1.60 tax) _____

Add postage & handling at **$3.00 ea.** _____

TOTAL $ _____

NAME

ADDRESS

CITY   STATE   ZIP

Please make checks payable to: Cookbook/Sholom Home Auxiliary
All proceeds from sale of cookbook will benefit Mount Sinai Community Foundation and Sholom Home
Auxiliary. For gifts, please include cards and a list of addresses. **Order online: www.sholom.com**

FOOD FOR SHOW
od on the go!

THE NEXT GENERATION

Cookbook/Sholom Home Auxiliary
3610 Phillips Parkway
St. Louis Park, MN 55426
(952) 939-1620

Please send me _____ copies at **$25.60 ea.** ($24.00 per book plus $1.60 tax) _____

Add postage & handling at **$3.00 ea.** _____

TOTAL $ _____

NAME _____

ADDRESS _____

CITY _____ STATE _____ ZIP _____

Please make checks payable to: Cookbook/Sholom Home Auxiliary.
proceeds from sale of cookbook will benefit Mount Sinai Community Foundation and Sholom Home
Auxiliary. For gifts, please include cards and a list of addresses. **Order online: www.sholom.com**

- -

FOOD FOR SHOW
od on the go!

THE NEXT GENERATION

Cookbook/Sholom Home Auxiliary
3610 Phillips Parkway
St. Louis Park, MN 55426
(952) 939-1620

Please send me _____ copies at **$25.60 ea.** ($24.00 per book plus $1.60 tax) _____

Add postage & handling at **$3.00 ea.** _____

TOTAL $ _____

NAME _____

ADDRESS _____

CITY _____ STATE _____ ZIP _____

Please make checks payable to: Cookbook/Sholom Home Auxiliary
proceeds from sale of cookbook will benefit Mount Sinai Community Foundation and Sholom Home
Auxiliary. For gifts, please include cards and a list of addresses. **Order online: www.sholom.com**

- -

FOOD FOR SHOW
od on the go!

THE NEXT GENERATION

Cookbook/Sholom Home Auxiliary
3610 Phillips Parkway
St. Louis Park, MN 55426
(952) 939-1620

Please send me _____ copies at **$25.60 ea.** ($24.00 per book plus $1.60 tax) _____

Add postage & handling at **$3.00 ea.** _____

TOTAL $ _____

NAME _____

ADDRESS _____

CITY _____ STATE _____ ZIP _____

Please make checks payable to: Cookbook/Sholom Home Auxiliary
proceeds from sale of cookbook will benefit Mount Sinai Community Foundation and Sholom Home
Auxiliary. For gifts, please include cards and a list of addresses. **Order online: www.sholom.com**